First edition
Copyright © 2010 Alastair Sawday Publishing Co. Ltd
Published in 2010 by Alastair Sawday Publishing
Reprinted in 2011

Alastair Sawday Publishing Co. Ltd,
The Old Farmyard, Yanley Lane,
Long Ashton, Bristol BS41 9LR, UK
Tel: +44 (0)1275 395430
Web: www.sawdays.co.uk

ISBN-13: 978-1-906136-35-2

Series editor: Alastair Sawday
Editorial Director: Annie Shillito
Editor: Ann Cooke-Yarborough
Writing: Alastair Sawday, Ann Cooke-Yarborough
Production: Julia Richardson, Rachel Coe,
Tom Germain, Anny Mortada
Maps: Maidenhead Cartographic Services
Printing: Butler, Tanner & Dennis, Frome, UK
Cover photograph: Atlantide Phototravel/Corbis
Cover design: Walker Jansseune

Photography

Lesley Chalmers
Château du Quengo
Clos Mirabel
Maison Rancèsamy
Pauliac
Château de Rodié
Domaine de Peyloubère
Gratia
Hôtel Cuq en Terrasses
Château de Lescure
Ferme des Prades
Auberge de Concasty
Auberge de Chassignolles
Château Clément
La Magnanerie
Domaine de Pélican
La Voix du Ruisseau
Le Couvent d'Hérépian
Villelongue Côté Jardins
L'Orri de Planès
Chalet Châtelet
Maison Coutin

Clémence Dubois
Chambres avec Vue
Château Les Bruyères
La Ferme de l'Oudon
Le Château
Les Moulins de Vontes
Le Bouchot
Hôtel Les Orangeries
La Montgonière
Château d'Alteville

Anne de Henning
Château de Craon
Château de la Motte
Le Clos de la Garenne
Château Ribagnac
La Chapelle
Ecolodge des Chartrons
Ferme de Félines
Le Moulin du Château
Château Juvenal
Auberge du Presbytère
Mas de la Rabassière
Mas de Cornud
Une Campagne en Provence
La Maison de Rocbaron

Andrew Johnstone
Château des Baudry
Château de Mayragues

Simon Williams
Can Llouquette

Go Slow France

Alastair Sawday
with Ann Cooke-Yarborough

Foreword
by Jean-Christophe Novelli

• Special places to stay

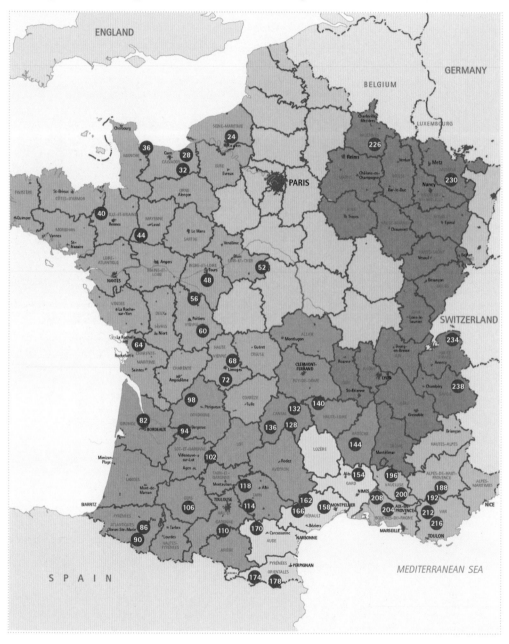

Contents

Foreword by Jean-Christophe Novelli

The idea of 'Slow' has its roots in Italy but could so easily have originated in France – convivial eating 'en famille' with lively chatter across the generations and food produced with love and care that respects and honours the 'local' and the culinary heritage. A civilised two-hour lunch break may not be as common as it once was but there are still places where it does exist and long may that continue.

French food cannot and should not be rushed – you really have to think ahead about the next meal. In France, this is not a burden, not a chore, just a way of life. A trip to the market to seek out seasonal treats – heaps of Étang de Thau oysters, truffles unearthed in the Périgord and glistening piles of cherries in June for a clafoutis, is a pleasure. So different from the drive-up whizz-round supermarket culture that we seem to have embraced here. Of course, I am not naïve enough to imagine that the whole of the country is tripping down to the market each morning – the supermarché has plenty of fans and, startlingly, France is loving le Big-Mac, but somehow they are still fiercely protective about their cuisine. I love that about France with each region upholding its

own traditions in wine, cheese, charcuterie and regional specialities, perhaps, cassoulet from Toulouse or the delightfully pungent cheese from Burgundy, Époisses.

My own inspiration came, like so many chefs, from watching my mother and grandmother at work in the kitchen. I still love to go back there and just opening the cupboards in my mother's kitchen takes me back – the aromas of fresh coffee, herbs, spices and vanilla are very evocative. She always makes my favourite dish of stuffed garden tomatoes – local lamb, St André onions, garlic and a sliver of Beaufort cheese sprinkled with smoked paprika – simple and delicious.

The people in this book understand what I am saying. And they are doing so much more than just creating great meals. They are slowing down, and if we have any sense we will slow down with them.

Jean-Christophe Novelli
www.jeanchristophenovelli.com

Introduction by Alastair Sawday

Before tackling this writing, I asked our author, Ann Cooke-Yarborough, what advice she had to give me. I think it is worth quoting her whole reply just as she wrote it:

The range of people and place is pretty amazing: from Alpine chalet to Pyrenean mountain refuge, goat farmers of the May '68 generation to landed gents in their utterly classic family château; a poet with yurts; left-leaning aristocrats who build organs and weave baskets when they're not tending their organic kitchen garden and shoring up their crumbling pile; a single woman running a simple B&B of immense human and cultural interest; a couple of sisters living quietly, organically, in the country and keeping up with all things international to feed the conversation with foreign guests at dinner; a Brit in Provence, whose bones have turned French through love of the place, people, food and wine; artists and historians, a collector of weighing scales, and one of the founders of an early gastropub (the Anchor and Hope in Waterloo) who left swinging London with his designer wife to bring up a family in saner, healthier climes: the remotest part of central France – need I go on?

I could add that there are people who live in a Regional Nature Park, who employ Wwoofers, belong to Slow Food, have an LPO (the French RSPB) bird sanctuary on their land, and get their seeds from Kokopelli, the renowned seed bank that is battling to save the planet's bio-diversity.

And several who are making use of EDF's micro-generation scheme to encourage private individuals, collective housing companies and businesses to produce their own renewable electricity using solar, hydro-electric or wind power. They sell the energy they produce to the power company for three to five times what they pay to buy it back through the grid. This price is guaranteed for twenty years.

They all use the term 'terroir' to express something intangible – the character of an area and its fruits – based on concrete ingredients: the landscape, the soil, the climate, things that grow there, how they are used to produce typical recipes, drinks – and even atmospheres.

Ann has a way with words, and with people. Researching this book has brought her close to

remarkable adventures and ideas. We could well have given this book another title: Meetings With Remarkable People. Here is a direct quote from one of them, saying little about himself but revealing an opinion or two:

"Our Belgian neighbour breeds organic veal on his Pyrenean hillsides. The method is as natural as it was a hundred years ago and a far cry from the hormone-heavy misery of battery-farm veal. Dairy farmers need female calves to make more milkers and to keep the cows producing milk. The male calves cannot be part of this long-term plan but are nevertheless raised on mother's milk and, once weaned, allowed out with the herd to graze in open pasture for a year before being sent to slaughter as organic veal."

The non-French inhabitants of this book are all converts, devotees of the concept of 'Frenchness', not nostalgically but intelligently

and thoughtfully. They have chosen to live there because of the space it gives them to be themselves, to pursue ideas of natural and non-exploitative living. Some of them have brought fresh ideas and energy to their communities. But the vast majority of the people we celebrate here are French, and it has been inspiring to learn from them of their values, dreams and successes.

Going Slow is a serious, lively, curious business. It means questioning everything you do, holding dear the notion that dawdling can be enriching, rejecting the current – and powerful – attractions of technology and fast travel. (I can almost hear Dorothy Parker at this point: "You can't expect me to drop everything and start counting sheep. I hate sheep!") It means taking another look at the virtues of simplicity in a world where everything is against it. It is strange how we know so much about our greatest needs, yet take so little heed of our own views. "The ability

shocking journey through the American food industry, revealing cynicism, waste and abuse on a huge scale, and comes to a very simple conclusion: eat food, not too much, mostly plants.

In other words, don't let the industry feed you rubbish, persuade you to eat too much of it, and above all don't let it persuade you to fill yourself with meat – most of which is awful.

That very simple conclusion above is at the heart of the Slow Food movement. Close to its heart is the injunction to eat local, preferably artisan, food, thus supporting producers who are not part of the gigantic food industry. The Slow Food movement is passionate about this and has galloped to the rescue of food varieties in danger of extinction all over the world. It matters that small-scale producers stay in business, in the same way that it matters that living species survive. They are all part of a vast ecological system that depends on variety. Our main food systems now depend on single plants, on species

to simplify means to eliminate the unnecessary so that the necessary may speak" (Hans Hofmann). In the case of Slow Travel, that means seeing and doing only as much as we really need to, as we enjoy. So, rather than see six cities, why not see one properly? Come to think of it, why not stay at home and have a deeper look at the city where we live?

Our approach to food illustrates the need for 'slowness'. One of the best books written about food is The Omnivore's Dilemma by Michael Pollan. It is a bible for those who think about food, yet he starts off by simply asking What Should We Have For Dinner? To quote from the book's excellent jacket: 'Such a simple question has grown to have a very complicated answer. We can eat almost anything nature has to offer, but deciding what we should eat stirs anxiety. Should we choose the organic apple or the conventional? If organic, local or imported? Wild fish or farmed? Low carb or low cal?' Pollan takes us on a

whose loss would imperil our survival, so dependent have we become on them.

So, the Slow movement in general is inevitably political – for it involves making choices that have wide-reaching effects. Eat mass-produced chicken and you are not only treating the chickens with contempt but yourself too. Fly far away for an exotic holiday and you are, as George Monbiot famously said, killing somebody. For that is what carbon emissions do when they cause climate change.

At the heart of this book, therefore, are some powerful messages. Each and every one of the people whose lives we reveal has a rich story to tell, a message to convey – and, above, all, an example to set. They are not all philosophers or powerful protagonists. Some are examples of how leading a quiet and slow life can turn you into someone whom others wish just to be with. Some dig their land and eat their own food in utter simplicity, but can inspire us by doing so. Others have thought things through in depth and tailored their lives to their philosophies. They are all, we think, very special.

Alastair Sawday

Normandy

Brittany

Western Loire

Loire Valley

Poitou – Charentes

Limousin

[THE WEST]

THE WEST

Brittany On the outer edge of France, between rocky coastline and barren hills, life was hard for most Bretons, whether peasants on stony ground or fishermen in dangerous seas (Brittany still brings in one third of the nation's total catch) though food comes more easily in the softer south where rhododendrons flourish: seafood and fresh vegetables (Brittany is famous for artichokes) are focal points of any meal in Brittany, and traditional pancakes make a welcome change from sandwiches.

Normandy Battered by wars throughout its history, Normandy is now a region of fashionable seaside towns, game-rich woods and cow pastures. Herds of the eye-patched cows that have made Normandy's reputation for cheeses are, however, largely condemned to sheds and high yields, as elsewhere. Wealthy Normans built big houses and for centuries poured fortunes into building cathedrals, abbeys and churches, too. All are worth travelling to see and Rouen's combination of gothic cathedral and half-timbered medieval streets is exceptional. Modern Normans serve the gods of taste with rich, elaborate recipes: it's no surprise that the digestion-boosting shot of Calvados between courses is called a *trou normand*.

The Loire France's longest river was one of the chief corridors of trade from Roman times until the age of steam. With the arrival of the Renaissance, king and court needed fresh territory to express the new humanist ideas and turned soft fertile Touraine into a great building site. Aristocratic, light-filled châteaux, manicured gardens, open minds and artistic refinement were now the ideal, not brute force. Rabelais, the formidably inventive writer and satirist (he gave us Gargantua), who was born in Chinon, was a priest, a lawyer, a doctor and a classicist.

Poitou - Charentes In Poitou, there's almost a goat's cheese for every village, little frescoed churches are a must and Poitiers, where the Saracen invasion was stopped in 752, is a splendid ancient-modern town. The Charentais are famous for their long, slow meals where course follows delicious course, starting with the famous Marennes oysters. They breed cattle, too, producing superb meat and cheese.

Limousin Although the Black Prince wreaked havoc in the area during the Hundred Years War, and frequent peasant revolts were cruelly repressed as France moved from feudalism towards central monarchy, the name Limousin summons images of mother-earth abundance beneath the chestnut trees. Since the discovery of kaolin here in 1768, the famous *porcelaine de Limoges* has been valued in all the great houses of Europe. Beyond the china factories, in green countryside, by myriad lakes and rivers, *limousine* cattle are prized for their meat, shown off at its best in the slow-cooking traditional recipes of rural France.

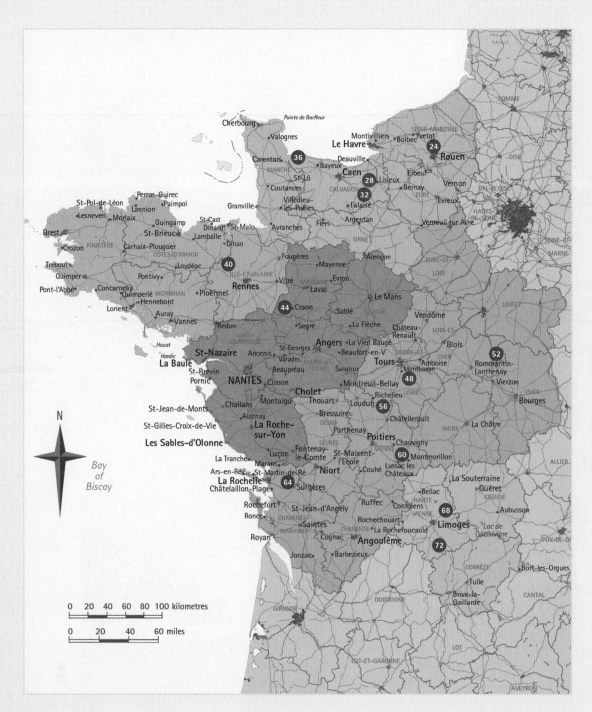

Pointe de Barfleur

Cherbourg
Valognes
Montivilliers • Yvetot
• Le Havre • Bolbec
Carentan • **24** Rouen
36 Deauville SEINE-MARITIME
St-Lô Bayeux • OISE
Coutances • Caen Elbeuf
Villedieu- **28** Lisieux Vernon
les-Poêles • **32** Bernay Evreux • VAL-D'OISE
Granville • Falaise EURE • HAUTS-
Avranches Flers Argentan Verneuil sur Avre DE-SEINE
St-Pol-de-Léon Perros-Guirec ORNE SEINE-ET-
Paimpol St-Cast Alençon MARNE
Lesneven Lannion Dinard St-Malo Fougères Mayenne •
Morlaix Guingamp Lamballe Vitré Evron EURE-ET-LOIR
Brest St-Brieuc Dinan **40** Laval Le Mans LOIR
Crozon Carhaix-Plouguer COTES-D'ARMOR ILLE-ET-VILAINE Vendôme LOIRET
FINISTÈRE Loudéac Rennes **44** Craon Sablé SARTHE
Tréboul Pontivy Ploërmel Segré La Flèche Château- LOIR-ET-
Quimper MORBIHAN Renault CHER Blois
Pont-l'Abbé Concarneau Quimperlé Angers • La Vieil Baugé INDRE-ET-
Hennebont Redon St-Georges Beaufort-en-V Amboise Romorantin-
Lorient Auray Varades Tours Montbazon **52** Lanthenay
Vannes LOIRE- Beaupréau Saumur **48** CHER Vierzon
Houat ATLANTIQUE St-Nazaire Ancenis MAINE-ET- Montreuil-Bellay LOIRE Bourges
Hœdic La Baule Clisson LOIRE Richelieu
St-Brevin NANTES Cholet Thouars Loudun **56** INDRE La Châtre
Pornic Montaigu Bressuire Châtellerault
St-Jean-de-Monts Challans DEUX- Parthenay
St-Gilles-Croix-de-Vie Aizenay La Roche- SÈVRES Poitiers Chauvigny ALLIER
Les Sables-d'Olonne sur-Yon VIENNE **60** Montmorillon
Luçon Fontenay- St-Maixent- Couhé Lussac les La Souterraine
La Tranche le-Comte l'Ecole Niort Châteaux GUÉRET
Marans Bellac CREUSE
Ars-en-Ré St-Martin-de-Ré Surgères Ruffec Confolens **68** Aubusson
La Rochelle **64** St-Jean-d'Angély La Rochechouart Limoges Lac de
Châtelaillon-Plage Roncé Saintes CHARENTE Rochefoucauld Vassivière
Rochefort CHARENTE Cognac Angoulême **72** PUY-DE-D
MARITIME Barbezieux CORRÈZE Bort-les-Orgues
Royan Jonzac Brive-la-
DORDOGNE Gaillarde CANTAL
GIRONDE Tulle
LOT
LOT-ET-GARONNE AVEYRON

N

Bay
of
Biscay

0 20 40 60 80 100 kilometres

0 20 40 60 miles

Special places to stay

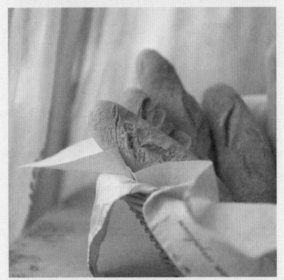

Chambres avec Vue

NORMANDY

"I don't grow vegetables, I don't join local groups, I am not an eco-warrior, in fact I'm not a warrior at all, and I'm probably rather 'fast'. But my way of life may represent a real ecology." So what is this ecology, where did it come from? Dominique's life has a dual focus: there's her gentle atmospheric house and the guests she receives here, and there's her work in Egyptian history and the thesis she is writing on distinguished twentieth-century Alexandrians, 'Heirs without an inheritance 1900-1970'.

"I aim to shape my life with a quiet discipline. I like wine, sharing and Sunday lunches, white tablecloths and stories I've heard a thousand times before. I like rituals. I love my freedom and the freedom of others." It has been a long flowering and she is enjoying its slow fruits: study, good conversation, and two months a year in the research centre at Alexandria.

For twenty-five years, she was a middle-class mother with a love of art and four full-time children in this fine townhouse. "A life of rich days spent close to home doing small things, caring for others and discovering that I liked holding open house." In due course, the family went off in different directions, Dominique stayed behind, and a free spirit was born.

She became a mediator for the housing authorities, in charge of persuading their tenants that they would like living where they were even more once the buildings had been renovated. "It sounds too easy but some people are suspicious of change of any kind." Then, during voluntary work in a Cairo orphanage, she discovered the fascination of Egypt. Deciding to become an archaeologist, she launched into the university life she had missed out on, learned to revel in erudition and solitude, and gradually made the house her own, with space for

her four children, seven grandchildren ("such a special relationship") and B&B guests.

She gave the television away and spread out the gleanings of her curiosity and love of people, particularly the uncharted lives of the lowly. Here are masses of books: Egypt, of course, in novel and textbook, poetry, books on other arts and artists, and the writers great and small who have become friends during quiet days alone. And a more modest kind of text, too, the scruffed-up exercise books of simple schoolgirls and boys of the early 1900s, in painstaking pen-and-ink, that she "saves" when she trawls a brocante or a jumble sale: "I can't bear to think of their valiant young efforts being thrown onto the public dump."

As well as books, there are hours of things to hold the eye: fine old oils and modern portraits (one of her nephews is a painter), simple line drawings, and her own and other people's family photographs. Dominique wholeheartedly adopts the characters and groups that take her fancy and several of her 'ancestors' wear the tarboosh. She knows the life story of every piece in those ranks of old glassware, china, biscuit tins and pen-knib packets, salvaged from a vanishing world. What could have been a mishmash of ill-assorted objects is harmoniously alive, as a guest wrote in this farewell:

"Each thing is imperfectly in its place,
even the light,
Like an intimate vibration.
And I stop, completely.
I put my hand on the books.
It all comes to me, without effort or will."

Below the balcony, the bushy, freedom-loving little garden, perfect for a quiet read, "is as it is," says Dominique, "I just give it a helping hand here and there".

Mont Saint Aignan is on a hill above Rouen and the higher you go in the house, the more you see of the piercing spires of the gothic cathedral below. Monet painted over thirty canvasses of its west end, each in a different mood, while Victor Hugo called Rouen, rich in

history, drama and religion, "the city of a hundred steeples and the debris of long-gone races." The steeple on the main tower is the highest in France, "it's even higher than the Great Pyramid of Cheops." After terrible wartime destruction, the little streets, timbered houses and glorious gothic monuments of the medieval town where Joan of Arc spent her last days (it was in 1431) have been restored. Dominique encourages her guests to walk down into town and take the time to get inside its skin, to see the details she knows so well and that people miss on the standard lightning tour.

"Doing chambres d'hôtes is an art, not a business," is her creed. She is an accomplished B&B artist, glad to live alone and yet share her time and space fully with others. Breakfast is a gastronomic reflection of her love of good things, a beautiful event where a new treat appears each morning – maybe Clafoutis Mimi (diminutive of Dominique) made with the season's fruits and a rich custard, or Crêpes au beurre d'oranger – and the conversation continues in this house of treasures, curiosities and lightly-borne erudition.

Dominique Gogny

Chambres avec Vue,
22 rue Hénault, 76130 Mont St Aignan
- 3 doubles.
- €60.
- Restaurant 1km.
- +33 (0)2 35 70 26 95
- chambreavecvue.online.fr
- Train station: Rouen

Château Les Bruyères

NORMANDY

The Harfaux family, with Philippe tireless in the front line, are a strong, vibrant and determined bunch. Having previously run a self-sufficient B&B in the Somme, they have been committed to leaving small footprints for years and their love of life embraces most of the natural world. Close attention to detail is how they do things, as any dish served in the dining room will prove.

When Philippe, once a marketing director, takes up the cudgels for a cause – be it horseflesh, energy-saving systems, fresh organic food or the Normandy apple – he is a powerful and intelligent force, firmly backed up his family. Michèle, constant, quiet, efficient, is his éminence grise; she oversees all the housekeeping and decides on décor and furnishings. "My taste and talent for hospitality run in the blood," she tells us, "since my parents and grandparents were Armenian and an Armenian cannot but provide a meal for any new arrival.

Sharing food is the foundation of life in harmonious society."

Julie, their daughter, has similar energy. During her training as a physiotherapist and masseuse, she looked after four horses while swotting for exams and came home with both the junior show-jumping championship and the professional diploma. At Les Bruyères, her talents are put to good use, and she also happens to be the mother of that golden-haired angel.

The Harfaux were born with horses, show jumping runs in the blood and they love the noble beast with a passion. The dozen or so mares in their stud deliver foals for the French show-jumper market – and rich manure for the vegetables; harvested rainwater provides for horses and garden; the family ride as often as they can and guests can stable their own mounts here.

"Food is far more than a simple necessity, it is an art", declares Philippe the master artist. He fell into

the magic potion as the child of a chef, his mother, who nurtured his sense of taste. Normandy has an age-old reputation for good food lovingly and richly prepared. Anything listed as 'à la normande' will be done with cream or cider or calvados – or all three – and cider, the product of those apples, is one of Philippe's culinary muses. He is even growing his own apple orchard for cider – hand-harvesting the apples, of course. "We are well known as ambassadors for the Normandy apple and for cooking with fresh produce only." He drives the whole process, from growing the vegetables in the château's beautiful organic potager to their perfect presentation on a plate in the dining room.

Ingredients must be in season. "What isn't growing in my kitchen garden won't be on your plate." He says his favourite occupation is that kitchen garden, all 4,000 square metres of it, where

> "Somehow, this family manage to make the whole place feel like a relaxed home, despite its size and smartness"

he feels that "being is more important than doing, even though there's a lot to do, because it is such a marvellous combination of things useful, educational and fun."

"What is a healthy vegetable?" he asks the group he is showing round, then answers his own question. "One that's in season. You won't see fresh tomatoes on our table until mid-July." He's a patient teacher, explaining all his plants, their names, tastes (guests are invited to nibble at flowers) and uses in cooking

In the kitchen, he is a recycling tyrant – "I want everything possible for my compost heap" – and the rules are draconian. But he won't have hens, not while running a smart hotel: "Have you ever heard the noise a cockerel makes? Totally incompatible with a quiet weekend in the country." So eggs and poultry come from the best local producer

of the moment. Fish must be sustainable, too. "I will only use animals from the sea that have reached adulthood."

Michèle, who has kept pace with his unstoppable drive for thirty-five years, tells of beach holidays where he can be found quietly writing the cookery book he plans to publish, rather than reading the year's bestselling novel like everyone else.

The Harfaux couple know and love fine art, European and Oriental, ancient and modern. The artists shown in the château are local and the day before an exhibition opens, Philippe can be found guiding the hanging operations, though with dogs as striking as theirs, you scarcely need painters, they are a form of living art, and with a grandchild like theirs, you surely need nothing but time for delight. Somehow, this family manages to make the whole remarkable and lovely place, big and smart as it is, feel like a relaxed home where slow living is a given, and a delightful one.

Philippe, Michèle & Julie Harfaux

Château Les Bruyères,
Route du Cadran, 14340 Cambremer
- 14: 8 doubles, 2 twins, 2 singles, 1 triple, 1 apartment.
- €120–€210. Singles €85. Apartment €290–€360.
- Breakfast €14. Dinner €39–€65. Wine €15–€50.
- +33 (0)2 31 32 22 45
- www.chateaulesbruyeres.com
- Train station: Lisieux

La Ferme de l'Oudon

NORMANDY

Flowers of all shapes, colours and scents, flowers inside and out, armfuls of flowers are here to greet you, even before you meet Patrick, Dany or their many animals. When this inspiring couple bought the Oudon farmhouse twenty-five years ago, the few hectares that came with it were defended by phalanxes of brambles, nettles, thistles and barbed wire.

The house was uninhabitable, too, having been left to fall into ruin by the eighty-year-old who last lived there. It had pondfuls of water, fertile soil, outbuildings with huge tumbledown personality, but it needed exceptional powers of imagination to believe it could become the wonderful watery universe it is today. Dany and Patrick continue to nurture it with loving care. "Our green bubble" is what Dany calls it.

Walt Whitman's song could be hers, with her passion for all living things:

'I believe a leaf of grass is no less than the journeyman of the stars,
And the pismire* is equally perfect, and a grain of sand, and the egg of the wren,
And the tree-toad is a chef-d'œuvre for the highest,
And the running blackberry would adorn the parlours of heaven.'
* ant

The Vesque family – Dany and Patrick have four children and three grandchildren – worked like Trojans, clearing, digging and stripping, revealing marvels such as the fifteenth-century pigeon tower, now a B&B room. The worn stone steps of its spiral staircase had been buried beneath layers of carpet, its alcoves and nesting holes walled up with breeze blocks and plastered over. There were other crumbling outbuildings to restore as gîte or

poolhouse using natural and local materials – stone and timber to match the originals – and Patrick's professional interior-design skills. The result is a mix of farmhouse rustic and cleancut contemporary, with much attention to comfort. Improvements continue: the spa and heated indoor pool "because that's what we appreciate when we ourselves are travelling"; the new modern room above it; a fourth room that has just been finished beside the new pool; and another weekend cottage with its own pond. Each cottage and bedroom is in its own tranquil world, independent of the others, and no detail is neglected.

Dany and Patrick both adore horses and guests can ride theirs or bring their own. The goats and donkeys are for company and decoration, the hens lay eggs for as long as they can then go into quiet retirement, the geese and ducks are for Christmas. Waste food goes to compost or the animals; waste water is treated and re-used because after 'home' treatment, their water is purer than the town water running from people's taps.

Outside her kitchen, Dany has a little 'priest's garden' for flowers, vegetables and herbs so she can just lean out and pluck what she needs when she needs it. She is immensely knowledgeable about plants (her parents were seed merchants) and nothing could be fresher than her vegetables, nor more organic. She's a people person, too, having been a nurse for thirty years. Guests have said that "kindness is her second name. She and Patrick make even the most reticent traveller feel at home. They will go so far as to help you speak French if you wish."

Cooking is as much a pleasure for them as the garden and the animals. They buy from local farmers, organic wherever possible, and Dany prepares her good-looking dishes with genuine enjoyment. She is one of those people who always have time, especially for others, and she considers that her totally reliable housekeeper, a pillar of the establishment, is a benefit for all. There's a kitchen garden for guests to use "but they often don't dare or don't know how, and I have to teach them to pick lettuces or dig spuds." With the multitude of unsprayed flowers in her garden, Dany is now learning bee-keeping, yet another item on the programme of balance and bio-diversity.

The enchanting Lavoir (washhouse), which can be used for either B&B or self-catering, is like being

in a Monet painting. Standing in its own hectare of garden, it is the epitome of what Patrick and Dany hoped to create, "a nature-watching haven, a place of peace for weary travellers to rest and recharge their batteries." The original washhouse beside the

> "Outside her kitchen, Dany has a little 'priest's garden' for flowers, vegetables and herbs so she can just lean out and pluck what she needs when she needs it"

pond was too ruined to save so they pulled it down and built this cabin with a deck out over the water. They then emptied the rubbish-filled pond, extended it and let it fill up again. And nature took over: the water lilies regrew, the frogs leaped back, the heron brought the first fish – which multiplied a thousand-fold – and the willows prospered. Three inseparable ducks now consider that deck is theirs, allowing the occasional guest to share.

"One of the best breakfasts in France" is served in the conservatory attached to the main house. This is another riot of plant life, some of the roots pushing down through the floor and across the border to pop up outside in Dany's little potager.

A well-known pianist who often stays here helped them choose the piano for this winter garden and impromptu recitals are not unknown. It is a house of harmony, laughter and goodness.

Patrick & Dany Vesque

La Ferme de l'Oudon,
12 route d'Écots, 14170 Berville l'Oudon
- 3: 2 doubles, 1 suite.
- €110–€180.
- Dinner €40, weekdays only. Restaurants 2km.
- +33 (0)2 31 20 77 96
- www.fermedeloudon.com
- Train station: Lisieux

Le Château

NORMANDY

What a woman! A phenomenal character, Dominique gathers all into her generous arms. As a fisherman's wife and mother of seven children, she quickly learned to run things on her own, he was so often at sea. She must have done it well, as her children still live in or near this pretty little fishing town whose houses face the north wind that sweeps over the sand-flats.

The coast of Normandy has not always been so peaceful. In the eleventh century, William Duke of Normandy was booted across the Channel by his cousin the King of France who urgently needed to be rid of William's quarrelsome warriors and his claims to the throne. This, the last invasion of Britain, is now seen as a positive influence on Anglo-Saxon civilisation (the Bayeux tapestry alone justifies that conclusion – don't miss it) but Anglo-continental rivalry was to remain a leitmotiv of European history and the fields of Normandy all too often its battleground. A large German gun battery was recently unearthed on the

cliff here; its last cannon was fired on D-Day in June 1944. Now families sunbathe on those beaches and fishing boats ply their (diminishing) trade beyond.

Some of Dominique's children became fishermen in their turn and one will always arrive with the day's catch. The mackerel caught the morning of our visit, filleted and grilled on the barbecue with a mustard sauce, were unforgettable in their sea-strength and freshness. Her tremendously convivial dinners are always constructed with the fruits of her labours in the garden, fish from the family boats or organic ingredients, where possible, from local producers.

There's often a Wwoofer* here, learning about organic gardening, French family life and the art of welcoming strangers. So the big country house hums constantly as children and grandchildren, cats and dogs – and guests – come and go.

Children adore Dominique, adopt her as their dream grandmother and hug her hard when they have

to leave. When she says "I'd love to be alone to catch my breath from time to time," it's hard to believe her, she has so much to share, so much to teach people. Anyway, she is unstoppably active, be it with the kitchen, the potager, the grandchildren or the village, adapting her pace to those around her.

Grannie Titine's Caramelised Rice Pudding

100 g rice
1 litre milk (fresh whole milk if possible)
55 g sugar

• Cook rice in milk. When cooked, add sugar and allow to melt.
• Pour into individual ramekins.
• Sprinkle with caster sugar.
• Heat a round iron over the gas flame, place it over sugar (or use a kitchen blowlamp) until sugar melts and covers rice, making caramel sauce.

"I live surrounded by nature and I try to slide through it as discreetly as possible. Our 'château' isn't a farm, just a big house with farmyard animals, including Marans hens that lay eggs so dark they look like Easter eggs." She has been an eco-activist since she was young. "I was eighteen in 1968 and ahead of the earth-awareness wave. For decades I felt I was rowing against the tide. I find it so restful to be 'normal' now." She has always grown her own fruit and vegetables and made hecto-kilos of jam and mouth-watering treats. Happy guests carry away the taste of unforgettable custards, rice puddings and chocolate mousses. "Our eggs come from the hens that peck and cackle in the field alongside the ducks and turkeys (who, of course, won't live beyond Christmas). The milk comes from our neighbour's organically-fed cows. We also have a couple of goats, but they're more for company than food."

The organic dairy farmer grazes his cattle on Dominique's land, in exchange for milk rather than money, and when more numbers and more species

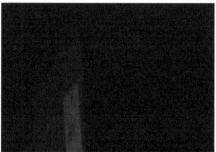

of wild birds arrive each season she is grateful to him and his respect for nature. "We have screech owls nesting in the attics, you can see them setting off to hunt at nightfall; there's been a falcon's nest under the eaves for years, with a new brood each summer; in the evening, we often see a fox hunting for its dinner, sometimes one of my ducks or hens..."

She and her former husband took over her family house twenty-five years ago and set about restoring it. "To start with, we made the usual mistakes with cement and plaster, but we quickly took to using more natural materials for rebuilding (mostly our own local lime, sand and gravel), then insulation (hemp) and finishes (limewash). Our first efforts at old-style painting with strange, experimental mixes of ingredients had some unexpected and unfortunate results that still show here and there... but the journey of rediscovery was fascinating and, at the time, learners and initiates shared their recipes – a sort of secret society. Now, of course, it's all on the internet, a gold mine."

Family house it is. There are pieces of fine old china, portraits of great-grandmothers in elaborate frames, pieces of fine old china, silver spoons, a natural elegance that informs the whole place, and yet it lives in simplicity and has nothing of the grand château intimidation. The house is a labour of love, each generation taking the time to live here and leave its mark.

* Wwoofer - see notes on p.242

Dominique Bernières

Le Château,
Chemin du Château, 14450 Grandcamp Maisy
- 4: 2 doubles, 1 twin, 1 suite for 5. €70-€85.
- €35 inc. aperitif & wine/cider (4 days per week); children €20. Restaurants within walking distance.
- +33 (0)2 31 22 66 22
- perso.wanadoo.fr/alain.marion/gbindex.html
- Train station: Bayeux

Château du Quengo

BRITTANY

"The challenge is to keep Quengo true to itself and a genuine family house: we steer clear of anything that smacks of fashion." Anne and Alfred gave up rewarding lives in Switzerland to throw themselves, without a penny, into the maddest project of all: saving her crumbling family estate – chapel, rambling old house, outbuildings galore, fourteen hectares of woods and ponds – and turning it into a "haven of peace and trust for people and animals without destroying its soul, or ours."

Seven years on, this amazing couple are sticking to their principles of Old is beautiful and Green is good. Quengo is a glorious, authentic experience, its rooms scarcely changed since the nineteenth century, apart from washing facilities added in corridors (Anne refuses to break through five-foot walls to make hotel-type bathrooms). One of the stunning wallpapers may be from the William Morris workshop. Others were discovered 'new', still rolled up in the attic.

Anne's family has entertained at Quengo for hundreds of years but life here has not been all smooth sailing. The French Revolution took its toll of the Breton nobility, some of them on the very steps of Quengo. "Quite right too," is her comment. All over the house are portraits and old photographs of the actors of this sometimes tumultuous family story and Anne

tells the tales with verve and a very personal take on national history. She is glad the revolutionary mob so damaged the dark and gloomy fifteenth-century building that a new façade had to be built with fashionably large windows.

Alfred's first trade is organ-building but he knows, loves and plays a multitude of instruments and can turn his hand to anything practical. Anne is an organic farmer and a basket weaver and they met at a musical event in Switzerland. When Anne's father died and the decision was made to come and run Quengo, Alfred wound down his business, "put some tools in a bag", and off they set. "Arriving at Quengo for the first time," he says "was like coming home," and he willingly surrendered his unpronounceable Austrian name in favour of his wife's.

He set up a full and fascinating organ-maker's workshop, told his contacts that he had "left the Alps for a ruined château in western France," and got down to work on the house. Winter at Quengo used to mean retiring to just three rooms wearing several layers of wool; rotten and warped, the 'fashionable' eighteenth-century windows let in the pervasive chill. Alfred is rebuilding them and has made second windows for all, saving the bubbly old glass – a vast project. He also gained one degree centigrade by simply making

moveable tailor-made plates to fit over fireplaces not used in winter.

His growing collection of old organ-builder's tools, some for use, some for display, is marvellous. Both of them will use an old tool if given the choice. Anne found an old set of scales in a dark cupboard and uses them to weigh the fruit and sugar that go into her kilos of preserves. She handles the correspondence, too, writing lively letters with her left hand and a fountain pen, while Alfred does all the emailing.

Driven by her love of farming, Anne left school to go to agricultural college. Disgusted to find that she was supposed to learn how to use harmful chemicals on land and livestock, she went to Ireland to unlearn those lessons with sheep on the open hillsides. Later, she found herself overseeing organic farms for a leading French certification body. This passion for animal welfare and all things organic still drives her. In good years, the kitchen garden produces enough for near self-sufficiency, and a healthy slug population along the way, the bane of her life. "I'm experimenting with beer traps but the most fragile plants can only be protected with expensive organic stuff."

Anne's second passion is basket-weaving, which she practises and teaches. "You can't learn this trade from books", she says. Having collected her willow, she soaks it in an antique stone bath then works with it in the natural light of the old servants' parlour. No servants nowadays, just this pair of hardworking, left-leaning aristocrats. "We do everything to give our guests a taste of château life – while we have none of it! When they arrive, I can honestly say 'thank you for coming, now I have a reason to sit down at last.'" Both she and Alfred speak fluent English.

These are generous, compassionate, down-to-earth people. "Our books, musical instruments and spaces are there for all to enjoy, our pasture for visiting horses to graze, our organic garden for guests to learn from." The most recent musical event at Quengo was a performance of Bach's suites for solo cello in the candlelit chapel: "utterly magical", said Anne. And their animals share themselves easily. Barrie, the enormous Leonberg, is sweet with everyone – grown-ups, children, other dogs. When Anne asks her

nicely, she takes guests down to the lake and back, a round trip through the woods and over the little bridge.

The estate is an LPO*, ASPAS* and GRETIA* nature reserve; birds and animals are learning that they are

> "Our books, musical instruments and spaces are there for all to enjoy, our pasture for visiting horses to graze, our organic garden for guests to learn from"

safe here, beyond the reach of gun-toting neighbours. (One of the 'privileges' won by the Revolutionary peasantry was the right for all to hunt with guns. Birds in France have a tougher time than elsewhere in Europe). Le Quengo is an oasis in every way.

* LPO, ASPAS and GRETIA -see notes on p.242

Anne & Alfred du Crest de Lorgerie

Château du Quengo, 35850 Irodouër
- 5 rooms. 1 cottage for 5-11.
- €50-€75. Cottage €420-€770 per week.
- Restaurants 1.5-5km.
  Guests may use kitchen & dining room.
- +33 (0)2 99 39 81 47
- www.chateauduquengo.com
- Train station: Rennes

Château de Craon

WESTERN LOIRE

'They treated us like royalty,' wrote one guest. The Château de Craon certainly has a regal air, its proud face looking down the stupendous sweep of formal gardens and up the next hill far away. It has even been called a 'little Versailles'. Although the barony of Craon has been part of French history for over a thousand years, the original medieval castle stood on another site, nearer the town. In the 1770s, his lordship the baron, marquess and count, knowing the townspeople loathed his lustful extravagance and rapaciousness and possibly feeling the imminence of the Revolution (it was just fifteen years away), left for a distant hill and built the neo-classical pile we see today, putting miles of parkland between him and the populace.

In two hundred and thirty years, the 'new' château has only once been sold, in 1827 to Loïk's forebears. Since then, his ancestors have handed it down, directly or sideways, from generation to generation, as he will do in 2020 to his eldest son. There has been

an inherited professional streak, too, in the family's long-standing involvement in the regional press. Loïk is a former journalist and now a newspaper owner, as his father was before him, and his son is already working on the paper.

The calm continuity of the place is so palpable that one feels Keats could have written the *Ode on a Grecian Urn* for Craon:

'Thou still unravished bride of quietness,
Thou foster-child of silence and slow time,
Sylvan historian, who canst thus express
A flowery tale more sweetly than our rhyme...'

The Guébriants say they watch people slow down visibly as they pass the gates, "and not just the speed of the car." They are profoundly attached to this fertile land and its traditions. "The Mayenne, one of the most rural of the French départements, is less vulnerable to

financial peaks and troughs," says Loïk. "The people here have their feet on the ground, even in the ground. Some call us stolid slowcoaches, some go so far as to use the word backward, but in their motorway madness the English go round us, the hole in the middle being our lovely Mayenne, and they are missing something of tremendous value. The Mayenne has so much slow, unspoilt nature, so many places to sit quietly on a bench watching the birds and the squirrels." Aware of how privileged he is, Loïk takes as much time as he can to do just this. "My indulgence here at Craon," he continues, "is planting trees, shaping shrubs and paths and, in my mind's eye, seeing our park in another hundred years' time, even more beautiful than it is now."

Hélène, a lawyer by training, mother of six children (the youngest is sixteeen and still at home in the holidays) and grandmother of six more, spends half her time helping local people with their

> "My indulgence here at Craon is planting trees, shaping shrubs and paths and, in my mind's eye, seeing our park in another hundred years' time, even more beautiful than it is now"

difficulties over land ownership, leases and successions. A city girl at the outset, she quickly came to love the country life that Loïk introduced her to and her gentle, attentive hospitality informs the genuine family atmosphere of this grand place. She wants the rooms to be comfortable yet appropriately supplied with antiques, engravings and old-style draperies. The bathrooms, modernised in the early 1900s, have a wonderful time-warp feel; yet everything works perfectly, "so," she says in proper French, "if it ain't broke, don't fix it."

They do what they can for the environment on the great estate but recognise that it isn't perfect. All lawn mowings go into the shrubberies to suffocate the

weeds "but how on earth are we supposed to deal organically with six kilometres of gravelled drives? I can't afford the twenty-four gardeners they had here before the war and I haven't yet found an alternative to chemicals, I'm afraid." The walled kitchen garden grows soft fruit and organic vegetables, "especially fashionable squashes, such as 'sultan's turbans'; we have a great autumn harvest and sometimes surprise our guests with a colourful present."

This potager, a hectare in area, is superb. No chemicals here. The elderly greenhouse is full of tomatoes, the walls covered in espaliered fruit trees, the vegetables laid in long rows, the beds glorious with flowers for cutting, the paths grassy green and the fruit bushes laden, although rabbits, to the gardeners' despairing amazement, manage to jump the metre-high metal gate into the beds. Loïk gathers the remaining fruits to make mountains of jam for family and guests.

Ornamental animals – ducks, geese, goats and the horse – roam freely in the park. As a guest at Craon, you too will be encouraged to stay a while, breathe deeply and take the time to explore the forty hectares of parkland and woods, walking those six kilometres of paths over rivers, round the swan lake, through meadows where cattle graze. There's even an ice house. "In those days, they didn't have electricity, the river froze in the winter, the snow lay long on the ground and they could stock the ice house for cool conservation all the rest of the year. We need to relearn things like this though, of course, the rivers don't freeze over any more. Time marches inexorably on, but more slowly at Craon..."

Loïk & Hélène de Guébriant

Château de Craon,
53400 Craon
- 5 rooms, 1 suite & 1 apartment.
- €120-€160. Single €100. Suite €240.
- Restaurants in village, within walking distance.
- +33 (0)2 43 06 11 02
- www.craoncastle.com
- Train station: Laval

Les Moulins de Vontes

LOIRE VALLEY

Fifteen centuries of green energy churn the river here. Wheels were being turned by the waters of the Indre in the sixth century, the so-called Dark Ages when the church was the sole depository of intellectual and technical knowledge and the abbeys owned and farmed great tracts of land. Vontes was recorded in 1010 as belonging to the Abbey of Cormery and in the twelfth century the monks built three water mills on this group of small islands in a bend in the river.

With its seven percent drop and weirs and mill races to harness its flow – one mill per mile – it was the most 'industrialised' river in the region. So efficient was the system that two of the three mills at Vontes went on grinding flour until 1964. Recycling is an old miller's tale, too. In hamlets along the river, the communal wells were generally built with a couple of worn millstones, one as the roof and one as the front step of the shelter.

The Degails' discovery of this magical place is a romantic story. During a weekend away from the frenzy of Paris, they were exploring the Indre in a rowing-boat, came round a corner among thick overhanging trees, and suddenly saw it, like a dream rising from the water. They landed and knocked on the door; it was opened by an astonishingly rough-looking squire wielding a shotgun and a triple-barrelled name. He subsequently became an ally, if an

eccentric one, and held off all other buyers until Jean-Jacques and Odile could afford to pay for Vontes in 1991. You, too, can take a boat on the Indre: they have two, one above and one below the weir.

Over the years, this pair of nature-lovers have researched the history, botany and eco-systems of their river world. It was they who set up the Esvres Environnement group to defend the fragile area, its bio-diversity and treasures, against a motorway project and other threats. "It was worth every minute; we discovered a rare butterfly that is protected worldwide, the 'cuivré des marais' (the marsh copper), and the authorities had to build the road through another piece of countryside."

The association is now drawing up an inventory of the flora and fauna in the valley, all the better to defend it. Unusually, the banks and the bottom of the River Indre are the property of the landowners, not the state, and the water belongs to no-one: this is the original Roman law.

No strangers to effort (they have bicycled across Syria and Jordan, trekked through Bhutan,...), Odile and Jean-Jacques worked tooth and nail to renovate their three millhouses. The tenth-century foundations of the Moulin du Nord had become so wobbly that saving them, and the eighteenth-century building they supported, took 240 tonnes of stone and 68m^3 of concrete. The three original mills

had been totally rebuilt after the devastating flood of 1770 that swept away all the mills along this stretch of river. Such a cataclysm is hard to imagine nowadays, the river is so contemplative and secret. Odile's love of this water is easy to understand. She boats on it, fishes in it, paints it and keeps her eyes open for the kingfisher and the rare orchid. Meanwhile, Jean-Jacques, a persuasive speaker, chairs nature-protection meetings, defends good causes, including a pro-Palestinian association, and reads a lot.

They both work hard in their flourishing kitchen garden, growing fruits and vegetables for table and larder, often from Kokopelli* seedbank seeds, and are especially proud of their broad beans. "We battle constantly with our gardener over Roundup.

> "They were exploring the Indre in a rowing-boat, came round a corner among thick overhanging trees, and suddenly saw it, like a dream rising from the water"

Rhubarb leaves boiled for half an hour deal just as effectively with greenfly and the mixture doesn't stink, unlike macerated nettle slurry, the pure green stuff that destroys the very scent of roses! We open our garden to the public in the summer, starting with the Rose Festival in June, and stinking roses wouldn't do at all. We have learned that the mill-lover (we get lots of them, they are bowled over by the three functioning wheels) is a particular type of like-minded human being, but we also enjoy showing schoolchildren how to find the hidden delights of nature and telling our stories to Loire valley tourists. The tourists are happy to see real people living real lives – a change from the ghosts conjured up in the grand châteaux." Odile's mother's enamel portrait of Marie Stewart, so briefly married to François II at Blois, is another small delight.

"We have declared this a No Hunting area, to protect my sensibility as well as the wildlife," says Odile, "I grew up in a hunting family but my first

shoot cured me of any interest. Early on at Vontes, we gathered up a family of orphaned ducklings and kept them in the bath in Paris for two weeks before releasing them back into the river. People thought we were mad but we still do it; we have three ducklings in care at the moment." They enjoy caring for guests, too. "We've travelled a lot in our lives and find it so rewarding to spend time with people from all countries and all walks of life; it feeds mind, spirit and soul." Breakfast, home-grown, homemade and organic, is served on a platform between the two weirs whenever possible. It is an important moment of the day and lively conversations may last well into the morning; occasionally, they are picked up again over dinner that evening in this watery paradise where the sounds of running water and birdsong keep you company night and day.

* Kokopelli - see notes on p.242

Odile & Jean-Jacques Degail

Les Moulins de Vontes,
37320 Esvres sur Indre
- 3: 1 twin, 2 doubles.
- €130.
- Restaurants 2.5km (easy bike ride) & 6km.
- +33 (0)2 47 26 45 72
- www.moulinsdevontes.com
- Train station: Tours/St Pierre des Corps

Le Bouchot

LOIRE VALLEY

Au passage les branches de groseillers sauvages nous agrippaient par la manche.
Wild blackcurrant branches clutched at our sleeves as we walked.
Le Grand Meaulnes Alain-Fournier

A couple of wizards in a bewitching forest? Anne and Jean-Philippe feel immensely rewarded when guests catch the magic of the Sologne. This is a land of forests and marshes where fairytales, little people and beliefs in the supernatural have always flourished. After its prime in the fifteenth century, when the court briefly made it fashionable and hundreds of new ponds were created to drain the swamps and provide revenue from fish farming, the region reverted to marshland, will-o'-the-wisps and deadly swamp fever.

The land and its inhabitants were shunned and left behind by the French Revolution and the march for 'progress', their traditions were called superstitions and their folklore preserved, paradoxically, by being beyond the pale. Only in the mid-nineteenth century, when Napoleon III became President then Emperor of France and led the court to his estate in Sologne, was the area rediscovered by wealthy city dwellers as a rich hunting ground. Using now-generous public funds the old drainage systems of ponds and channels were restored for healthier land and air and the

bourgeoisie built some splendid hunting lodges.

Strong, intelligent and sensitive, "dreaming since childhood of a place where men, animals and nature could live in peace together," Anne the Parisienne took to Sologne life like an eagle to the air, and that includes the old stories of myth and magic that she loves to tell. Storytelling evenings often happen here, led by her or inspired by experienced friends. A passionate swimmer, particularly with dolphins, Anne is a practising lawyer and wildlife photographer. She is in her element at Le Bouchot, surrounded by her happy menagerie. If you're lucky you'll be there when the peahen is teaching her chicks to fly, taking off from a low roof to go and roost in safety in the trees. Anne's own chicks are three bright little girls, Charlotte, Mathilde and Lucille, who are fully part of the joyful, thoughtful community that is Le Bouchot, with cousins and friends often boosting the tribe. Visitors' children love it here, of course, and easily join the gang.

Jean-Philippe, another strong, committed character, is a naturalist and writer who guides expeditions, often for film or research projects, all over the world – the Amazon, the desert, Brazil. He used to run a dolphin protection group and now helps train eco-guides. His environmental crusade was triggered by a meeting with

Cousteau and one of his greatest friends is a desert Tuareg who comes to stay from time to time. His contacts with empty spaces and less frantic lifestyles have brought him a buddha-like philosophy, a deep respect for mother earth and a love of cooking. His eco-consultancy company, based here at the farm, provides expert guidance on sustainable building and natural materials and is currently working on an eco-village project.

Their passion for dolphins brought these two together and it seemed natural that they should leave Paris and start a new life "in an area where nature and culture lived side by side"; less natural,

> "Here we could bring our childhood dreams down to earth, rehabilitating the farm with natural materials and creating a place to live a nourishing family life"

perhaps, that they should choose an extraordinarily filthy, rundown farm way out among the old swamps. "But," as Anne says, "the three-hundred-year-old buildings were sound, the classic Solognot four-square plan was simple and harmonious, the natural environment exceptionally unspoilt and the history deeply human. During the occupation, for example, the Sologne was on the border between the occupied and the free zones and the farm was a refuge for Jews." Jean-Philippe spent eight months cleaning the place and revealing its beauties; the warm brick walls shimmered again in their rightful colours, the timbers glowed brown not black, the floors sparkled with life instead of dismally reflecting the darkness. "Here we could bring our childhood dreams down to earth, rehabilitating the farm with natural materials and creating a place to live a nourishing family life. We have all the animals we wish for and can welcome others into our haven

of nature and environmental protection." They did all the rebuilding, renovating and decorating themselves, it is all hand-made, simple and entirely unfrilled and if the furnishings are rudimentary, the company is inspiring and the food delicious.

Let them guide you round the reed-bed water treatment system, the wattle and daub construction, the hemp insulation, the wood-fired heating, the organic potager and orchard – "our edible forest of old-variety fruit trees" is how Jean-Philippe describes it – and all the creatures that feed on and nurture the farm. The estate had been stripped of trees and all the plants demolished by weedkiller. Anne and Jean-Philippe planted so many trees, bushes and hedges that the wild birds have flocked back. In May one particular spot, where they put in two-hundred-year-old-variety shrubs, is an explosion of colours. Anne spends hours digging, sowing, pruning and weeding, "but no more than necessary," she says, "because lots of so-called weeds are useful, either in the garden or in the kitchen." She and Jean-Philippe work towards permaculture on bio-dynamic principles, mulching, sowing and treating according to that special calendar.

It is difficult not to be inspired by the way these two have shaped their lives. Most of us go no further than dreaming, but at Le Bouchot nothing seems impossible.

Anne & Jean-Philippe Beau-Douëzy

Le Bouchot,
Route de Chaon, 41300 Pierrefitte sur Sauldre
• 3: 1 room for 3, 1 for 4, 1 suite for 2-7. Gîte for 4-6.
• €55-€75.
• Dinner with wine, €25. Restaurant 2km.
• +33 (0)2 54 88 01 00
• www.lebouchot.net
• Train station: Lamotte Beuvron

Château de la Motte

POITOU - CHARENTES

The Latin motto over the door of the Château de la Motte tells us that 'The door of this castle is never closed to an honourable man.' "Our philosophy exactly," says Jean-Marie. "In 1998, after many travels, living in Quebec and the wild Yukon, bringing up six children, moving back to France, we thought: 'Let's buy a château and have lots of people to stay.' La Motte had everything we wanted: the masculine (it's part-fifteenth century), the feminine (part-eighteenth century), a need for serious renovation, a non-existent garden, a landscape fashioned by human industry. Coming from the diligent tribes of Alsace and Lorraine, we both love hard work and sharing and we both want to grow and serve healthy gourmet food. The château and garden have been our project for the last ten years and we've enjoyed every bit of it."

When Jean-Marie's work in textiles (he was once a scientist) took him to Quebec, Marie-Andrée left her job as a surveyor and emigrated with him. She soon decided that she could "do better than the so-called French restaurants {they} dined at," and opened a place of her own. Three chefs later, she took over the cooking, paving the way for her table d'hôtes. "We care deeply about the food and wine we serve, which must be organic or local wherever possible, and dinner at our big table is the highlight of the day. A convivial atmosphere is as important as good food, of course. People relax with each other over aperitifs in the salon then talk history and legends, architecture and personal stories at table. They love hearing Jean-Marie's history of the château, too."

He blithely announces that he has a "photograph" of the man who owned the castle in 1408 and thinks the house ghost must be a knight who took refuge here in 1434, seduced the lady of the manor and was murdered by her husband. The Black Prince fought some battles in the area and his closest advisor, the much-loved Sir John Chandos,

was mortally wounded at Lussac bridge in 1380. Sir John's sword and a pot of silver were found buried at the spot centuries later. "From the marauding Vikings and the Normans, through the invading Arabs to the Anglo-French Plantagenets and the Hundred Years War, these stories – violent, funny, tragic – weave a tapestry that includes all of us Europeans." The château is the perfect backdrop to such dramas, the final flourish being Jean-Marie's absinthe, heated in old-fashioned absinthe spoons. "When I inherited them, I had no idea what they were for; now they are put to proper use again."

Jean-Marie and Marie-Andrée say "We are Slow by birth. As country children after the war, we knew that the meanest object, the smallest piece of fruit was valuable. A crust of stale bread would be kept for the animals or our soup, papers were kept for lighting the stove, peelings for the compost heap. More recently, we have grown disgusted by contemporary consumer frenzy. Being responsible means sourcing locally and doing things by hand."

The Bardins' commitment to DIY goes well beyond the normal call of duty. Marie-Andrée turns her hand to anything from tiling to embroidery, furnishings to stone carving (one fireplace is her own work) – and always with a smile. What she doesn't do, Jean-Marie does: stained glass and carpentry, picture framing, liqueur and aromatic wine mixing (his specialities are wine with purple basil or fennel-flower or 'seeds of paradise', and sloe gin). Once the major work on the fabric of the building was finished, they decorated the whole château with homemade hangings and draperies, their grandmothers' watercolours, some superb family antiques and shelves stuffed with books on plants, medieval and renaissance architecture and past civilisations.

Then came the garden. The fruit of much research and back-breaking work, this is a marvellous creation, with a medieval potager – called the Garden of Light – that supplies a huge variety of vegetables and herbs for cooking and healing, some resuscitated from medieval oblivion. There are two orchards of fruit trees and bushes, a

sheltered Garden of the Senses in the old moat where flowers are grown for innumerable vases, and a witch's garden on the edge of the property for magic plants such as belladonna and mandrake. Their

"We care deeply about the food and wine we serve, which must be organic or local wherever possible, and dinner at our big table is the highlight of the day"

harvests of proteiform squashes and sweet red fruits are dazzling, they make pounds of jams and preserves, their own vinegar and walnut oil, and even several mustards from their own plants. Should you be wondering what their secret is, they will, at least, admit to using tons of horse manure each year.

Jean-Marie & Marie-Andrée Bardin

Château de la Motte,
86230 Usseau
- 4: 1 twin, 1 triple, 2 suites.
- €80–€130.
- Dinner with wines, €30.
- +33 (0)5 49 85 88 25
- www.chateau-de-la-motte.net
- Train station: Châtellerault TGV

Hôtel Les Orangeries

POITOU - CHARENTES

With Les Orangeries, Olivia and Jean-Philippe have created a resoundingly green hotel, the first in France to win the Écolabel Européen stamp of approval and a wonderful place to bring up their three young children. As an architect, Jean-Philippe is dedicated to planning and building sustainably. "It isn't always easy but people are at last beginning to see that it's not just about 'being kinder to the planet', that it makes economic sense, too." Starting with his beloved grandmother's house, the project gradually took in six more eighteenth-century roadside terraced houses and their gardens. "The result," says Olivia, "once you are away from the road, is a hectare of harmony in the middle of the little town." You know it as soon as you see the swimming pool, its deep wooden deck, plain stone walls and baskets of plants, all quiet beneath the trees. The plan was initially given shape by those magnificent old trees, the fruitful orchard and the hectare of patchy land, now transformed into lovely gardens. Some rooms overlook the gardens, others give onto the road (not for the deeply noise-sensitive, these, despite double-glazing).

They began ten years ago as they meant to go on, with the most eco-friendly approach feasible, using hemp and lime, timber and stone, old rather than new whenever possible. "We wanted to use

materials that did the least harm to the environment and would grow more beautiful as they aged." The heatwave of 2003 and its tough water restrictions triggered a further water-saving drive and an 8,000-litre rainwater tank was built. "It costs more than it will save in decades but we do it anyway!" Olivia's enthusiasm for her house, children and guests is infectious; her constant search for greener ways of doing everything is an eye-opener.

As a guest at Les Orangeries you can be highly eco-virtuous. Arrive by train to be met by a handcart to wheel your stuff to the hotel: it takes five minutes. Bask in the lush, chemical-free garden with a cup of organic fairtrade tea before settling into your elegant, uncluttered bedroom. In a bathroom lined with timber recovered from old railway coaches, you shower with refillable organic shower gel in harvested rainwater, noting the three different waste bins as you do, then set off to the gourmet bio-restaurant where Olivia will hand you a small Slow menu of exquisite dishes made with the freshest local and organic ingredients.

After the loving conversion of the buildings, Olivia's dream was to make the restaurant both eco-responsible and captivating, a place where people could (re)discover the real taste of things. The kitchen garden was producing good harvests; the staff were

totally involved in the eco-ethos; the right chef would bring it all together. It took time but she eventually found the talented young Marc Lindenlaub to lead her committed kitchen team. "It's an extraordinary lesson in humility: the garden won't grow what doesn't belong here and the chef won't cook what he doesn't like." It is his suggestion that the big dining-room fireplace be used to smoke hams and sausages.

Marc likes giving time to traditional country dishes such as bœuf bourguignon, coq au vin, pot au feu, all using lowly cuts of meat and stacks of vegetables. He is a back-to-the-potager man and in winter produces seasonal "meals of roots," reminding guests that, one Good Friday in the sixteenth century, King Henri III was served just such

> "Bask in the lush, chemical-free garden with a cup of organic fairtrade tea before settling into your elegant, uncluttered bedroom"

a 'penitential' dish and found it utterly delicious. Each menu lists no more than two choices per dish, with sources described in detail, so that the cooks can concentrate totally and waste is minimal. Guests' plans can help, too. "It's incredible that some guests can't decide whether or not they will be dining in! A carrot takes six months to grow and they can't take two minutes to make up their minds about dinner," says Marc.

Responsible sourcing is a constant preoccupation. Olivia demands suppliers' carbon footprints. "Filet mignon (pork fillets) used to be our speciality but our local producer, whose free-range pigs have little wooden huts and no electricity, reminded me that one pig produces two fillets and he couldn't slaughter his whole herd for just one of our Sunday lunches. So we stopped doing filet mignon and kept our virtuous producer. Our pigeon-breeder gave up his organic

certification because it meant flying feed in from far away, a total contradiction."

Her current campaign drive is to find good organic wines. "Except Bordeaux, because the damp climate makes it virtually impossible not to spray against mildew. Organic growers have to trust the grapeskin's natural yeast, the holy grail of pre-chemical days. They take huge risks producing natural wines without doctoring or disguising anything and bad years are disastrous for them."

The next day, borrow electric bikes and discover the gentle, bucolic countryside; there are 850 kilometres of tracks to choose from. Or take Olivia's advice on local sight-seeing circuits involving the least driving: she's worked it all out for you. With all this, she still finds time to be with her children. "I think we have found the recipe for a unique cocktail of place and staff, guests and family and the eco-nurturing philosophy that binds them all. People certainly seem to find it an excellent tonic."

Olivia & Jean-Philippe Gautier

Hôtel Les Orangeries, 12 avenue du Docteur Dupont, 86320 Lussac les Châteaux
- 15: 11 doubles, 4 apts for 4-5 (no kitchen), €70-€185.
- Breakfast from €12.50. Dinner from €22. Wine from €18.
- +33 (0)5 49 84 07 07
- www.lesorangeries.fr
- Train station: Lussac les Châteaux

Le Clos de la Garenne

POITOU - CHARENTES

The emblem of the Charentes region is the snail, its most renowned product is the carpet slipper (though others might say cognac...) and it is said that drivers here are so slow off the mark that traffic lights are regulated on a longer changeover than anywhere else in the country. So when Patrick and Brigitte found that their high-stress jobs in sales and industry had become alienating and their three daughters were growing up at speed in an urban jungle, their thoughts turned to Charente Maritime, the cradle of Brigitte's family, where her grandmother still lived. They found a big dilapidated country house with four hectares of walled and wooded grounds and, as they both loved entertaining and feeding friends and family, they decided to do 'green' chambres and table d'hôtes.

All went slowly but surely for two years, children and animals thrived, the first lambs were born, the first guests were enchanted. Then, at

Christmas 1999, in a night of darkness and horror they will never forget, a mighty hurricane threw down ninety percent of their trees – "our primeval forest" as they called it – and salt-laden winds burnt the leaves of those left standing. "Fortunately, family and animals were untouched but the damage to roofs, paths and the perimeter wall was monstrous. We almost gave up."

They have been clearing and rebuilding for ten years, leaving the wild part to regenerate itself naturally. "That's where nightingales and owls have come back to live and breed," says Patrick, "and migratory wood-pigeons *palombes* take refuge from the shotguns. So much so, in fact, that they've stopped migrating and stay here eating acorns all winter – and occupying the nesting boxes I put up for the hoopoes."

La Garenne is a member of the Ligue de Protection des Oiseaux (LPO*) and Patrick enjoys

educating townies who can't tell a pigeon from a pheasant. Meanwhile, the local woodmen have helped clear the fallen timber, taking payment in kind and stacking the family's woodpile with decades of fodder for the big wood-burning stove in the main house.

Since the storm, they have planted an orchard of over twenty trees; this is where the Maran hens live and lay their dark russet eggs. Tomatoes grow among the dahlias, raspberries among the rose bushes. All other ingredients for Brigitte's succulent regional dishes come fresh from the local and organic stalls at the glorious Surgères market, from their own sheep – "lamb from anywhere else just cannot compare with Agneau de la Garenne" – or from the hedgerows.

Since coming 'home', Brigitte has been tutored by her grandmother in all things rural and regional. The family traditions included taking the handcart to gather grass for the rabbits and picking all sorts of other wild plants along the way: dandelions, nettles, sorrel,... and, as a youngster, she was initiated by the old country folk in local lore, patois, stories and songs. She often entertains her guests with the old tales and her happiness, shared with

Patrick, at being here with her family and her animals (boxers Vador and his son Excel, and donkeys Dédé and Fanfan) is catching. The three young teenage girls can also draw on a rich store of memories of guests down the years. Brigitte's hymn to her female forebears says:

> *You are the inexhaustible fount of the empirical*
> *lore of woman, family and life that flows*
> *towards other daughters, nieces and cousins,*
> *future grandmothers, great-grandmothers,*
> *great-great-grandmothers.*

Patrick delights in his country life, too, and is passionate about people, wildlife, history and, curiously, weighing scales. He has over two hundred of these and is hoping to create a museum in an outbuilding. He also collects comic strips, especially those with a science-fiction, historical or humorous bent – hence his animated website. He serves his Pineau des Charentes aperitif with gusto, calling it "a powerful ally that helps to untie the tongues of the shyest." And he laughs a lot. At the big dinner table, as the party tucks into Atlantic fish, local mussels or oysters, poultry, rabbit or

home-grown lamb, he pours wine without stint, remarking that the Belgians call this "living like God in France." They both feel that "making our own jams and pastries, simmering seasonal artisan

"The family traditions included taking the handcart to gather grass for the rabbits and picking all sorts of other wild plants along the way: dandelions, nettles, sorrel..."

produce and sharing the result with people from all walks of life, well, it just seems obvious and natural, yet some of our contemporaries appear to think it's some great achievement!"

Inside the house, high elegant rooms, renovated with natural and recycled materials and furniture, have a fairytale quality; children love them. Original features such as fireplaces, ironwork and panelling have been highlighted with tender attention. Brigitte's brother, a sustainability architect, has

designed a panoramic study and a summer kitchen with a vast barbecue while a tumbledown outbuilding has become a suite for guests with physical or mental handicaps. Charente Maritime is ahead on disabled facilities and the tourist office provides special equipment for wheelchairs that allows them to move along the great network of hiking and cycling paths.

La Garenne is a place of happiness and harmony and, at ninety-seven, Brigitte's grandmother is rejoicing in, and adding to, its success.

*LPO - see notes on p.242

Brigitte & Patrick François

Le Clos de la Garenne, 17700 Puyravault
- €69 for 2, €129 for 5. Tournesol €400 per week.
- 4 + 1: 1 double, 1 family room for 3-4, suite for 6, cottage for 5. Tournesol cottage for 2.
- Dinner with wine, €25.
- +33 (0)5 46 35 47 71
- www.closdelagarenne.com
- Train station: Surgères TGV 5km

Château Ribagnac

LIMOUSIN

Successful lawyers in the City, with young children whom they saw too little of, Patrick and Colette were vaguely thinking of "downshifting to regain control of (their) lives and environment"... later. On holiday in France in 2003, they visited Ribagnac on a whim (it was too big, too daunting, too soon), and were hooked. "It desperately needed rescuing, and we needed an excuse to buy it. Such warmth breathed out from the neglected old place that it was irresistible and we felt instinctively that it was meant to be the heart of a community." So to the rescue they came, and for six years have been working harder than they ever did in London.

In this land of clear lakes, limpid rivers and woods teeming with wildlife, among gentle curves and quiet pastures, the new arrivals discovered a genuine co-operative spirit and happily joined the system. "When someone has too much of something, they share it with neighbours, be it carrots, game, a place for hay, a pasture for animals, or simply a helping hand." They also join in a hilarious traditional 'competition' to force one's surplus on others. "If my tray of tomatoes is bigger than yours, you have to take mine. If you have yellow courgettes and I only have green, I have to accept your yellow ones."

The kitchen garden had fed the estate's inhabitants for centuries but needed huge amounts of work, much of it provided by willing Wwoofers*. Some 600m² are now cultivated for family and guests and the château is almost self-sufficient during the season. They use organic seeds and cuttings from older varieties, have learned all about green manures and such things as evil-smelling, super-effective nettle fertiliser-cum-pesticide, and they gather great harvests of fruit for jams, liqueurs – and the neighbours, of course.

Colette's dinner menu will be inspired by what the potager is producing and what looks good at the

market that morning. Limousin beef and lamb are renowned for their quality, the region's rivers are rich in fish and pasteurised cheese is hard to find here, a definite clue to how people choose their food. There will always be lots of fresh vegetables, even in the children's early supper, when they try things they would have refused at home. Grownups can then get to know each other over dinner and glasses of Patrick's careful choice of wines, many of them organic, and water from the estate's icy-cold spring.

"Work on the château will never be finished," says Patrick. "We have had so many energy studies done, but it's difficult to be efficient in an old building like this." They heat with wood where

> "Colette's dinner menu will be inspired by what the potager is producing and what looks good at the market that morning"

possible (eight hundred trees fell in the monster gale in 1999, so they have fuel for several years yet); their outbuilding conversions are more amenable than the château to the single big wood-burner solution. "Doing things right, such as not using pesticides, MDF or PVC, re-roofing the chicken house with one-hundred-and-forty-year-old slates from the château, using reclaimed timber to rebuild floors, is harder work but it's so much more rewarding. In the City, we would see a tower block go up in two months; trees are slower, last longer and are more useful."

To the Bergots' amazement, the local historical society had never been allowed to see the château, despite its importance to the area's history. The society now have a dossier about it and produce stories from its past for their newsletter. The house and gardens, reclaimed from a forest of brambles and all those fallen trees, some of them giant one-hundred-and-fifty-year-old American oaks, are now open for the annual Journées du Patrimoine,

attracting an astonishing six hundred visitors in one day. Among other things, people come to admire the great trees that survived the battle with the winds: very old blue cedars, copper beech, tulip and magnolia trees, oak and American oak, acacia, lime trees and sequoia, as well as fruit and nut trees – a splendid array.

Sometimes called the French Lake District, the countryside has inspired many painters, including Corot, who was particularly drawn to the Creuse valley. The paintings in the honeymoon suite at Ribagnac were once attributed to him... then not.

George Sand introduced the Impressionists to her beloved Limousin in the 1800s and Colette could be quoting her when she says: "Setting off for school early in the morning is a gift; the lakes are calm and beautiful and the skeins of mist that lie along the valleys make it all so mysterious." Neither she nor Patrick has an ounce of regret for that life-changing decision, especially as they watch the children grow up with a sense of fitting into the scheme of things and naturally expecting to give something back. "It may be an endless job, like all old buildings, but we are proud of what we have done, for ourselves, for our children, and for the crumbling wreck and wild parkland we have saved. The place has been here for four hundred years so we feel privileged to be passing through, adding something, then leaving it for another half millennium"

* Wwoofers - see notes on p.242

Patrick & Colette Bergot

Château Ribagnac,
87400 Saint Martin Terressus
- 5 suites for 2-5.
- €90-€160.
- Dinner with wine, €45.
- +33 (0)5 55 39 77 91
- www.chateauribagnac.com
- Train station: Limoges

La Chapelle

LIMOUSIN

True children of May '68, Patrick and Mayder (pronounced my-dare) have stuck to the ideals they adopted in those days of optimism and new opportunities and have developed their particular philosophy of social cohesion, honest activity and frugality. They were students when they first became aware of the destruction wrought by industrialised agriculture and the takeover of farming by capital and business. They became eco-warriors and still live by the same convictions forty years on.

They did what they could afford, found a smallholding in lovely, lyrical Limousin and Mayder stayed in teaching (but will retire in two years' time, to her relief). The local traditions of cattle and cereals require high investment and were beyond their reach; a market garden was not viable, the land here being all clay. So they took up goat farming, Patrick learning the ropes and how to make better and better cheese. Goats were not the most obvious choice, either, as they need light and air and the region is characterised by shady woods and a clay soil that prevents water from draining. The clay has its uses, however: the superb buildings round the corner were an old tile factory and local roofs are a festival of shapes and patterns in terracotta.

After researching organic methods, they opted for Rudolf Steiner's bio-dynamic approach to farming as the most holistic.

"Bio-dynamics," says Patrick, "makes it much easier to cope with the difficult soil and produce more 'luminous' feed for our goats. As directed by Steiner, I use 100g of cow dung sufficiently diluted to treat one hectare of clay land and over time it drains far better. As fertiliser, I add 4g of powdered quartz to a hayfield at sunrise and I harvest as much hay per bio-dynamic hectare as my neighbour gets on his chemical-fertilised hectare. These powders have each previously spent six months in a cow's horn buried in a field, pulling in the earth forces. It sounds like magic but it works and that's all I need."

The inspirational Steiner prescribed all this in detail in 1924 in his 'Lectures to Farmers'. "He saw and knew things way ahead of his time. No-one knows where the knowledge came from nor how it works but he was right; my goats are the living proof. I treat them once a year for intestinal parasites and they never have worms, my neighbour's lambs are treated once a month and have chronic gastric trouble."

So they came from Normandy in 1978 with ideas and methods that were aeons away from those of the locals, yet they were well received. Why? "Oh," says Mayder, "the neighbours loved us. When they saw us arriving with two small children, they knew the village school would be saved. But they thought we were mad and heading

for disaster with our organic goats. Without generations of land ownership behind us we will always be foreigners but they now admit that we weren't mad, even though maximum income has never been our aim." And Patrick, ever the social ideologist, adds: "We stuck to our ecological ideals through thick and thin and created good lasting relationships with our neighbours. We believe that, to succeed, any project must be anchored in the social environment." They find it pleasing to reflect that non-intensive Limousin farming was considered old-fashioned, even backward, for decades. The region is now held up as an example because its land and resources are better preserved and healthier than those that have been drenched in chemicals.

B&B was fairly revolutionary in the Haute-Vienne at that time, too. "We were just fifteen doing B&B thirty years ago, now there are a hundred and forty." Mayder does the rooms and the simple meals, finding it fits easily with her teaching

> "As fertiliser, I add 4g of powdered quartz to a hayfield at sunrise and I harvest as much hay per bio-dynamic hectare as my neighbour gets on his chemical-fertilised hectare"

timetable. They both love the conviviality, the opportunity to meet people from many walks of life and to introduce townies to life in the country. "Some people haven't a clue what a goat or a hen looks like," says Patrick. "They find it exciting to see live food close up. As for farmers, those of my age remain deeply resistant to change but the younger generation are becoming aware of the need to work together to protect our finite resources. Our daughter Céline will soon be taking over the farm. She and her husband are building a straw house nearby and she's going to grow organic fruit. Goats are too demanding for her! It's true that you can't

just leave them and go off on holiday, but Mayder and I will keep a few for our own milk and cheese and continue with the B&B – and we'll have lots more time to enjoy our guests."

As well as the flock of goats and a few pigs, Patrick tends fifty Limousin laying hens – he weighs and rubber stamps every single egg by hand – and their cockerel. This proud gentleman is a 'fishing cock', so called not because he goes fishing but because the fine feathers of his neck are ideal for making fishermen's flies. "These cocks are so valuable that they are traded at auction; it's really quite a surprising event."

Beyond the fence, there are tribes of foxes, deer and wild boar; a census done in 2008 recorded thirty-five bird species in nearby Fayat forest: off the beaten track it may be, but not unsung.

Patrick & Mayder Lespagnol

La Chapelle,
87380 Château Chervix
• 4: 3 doubles, 1 triple.
• €45.
• Supper €10. Wine from €5. Guest kitchen.
• +33 (0)5 55 00 86 67
• gite.lachapelle.free.fr
• Train station: Limoges

Aquitaine   Midi - Pyrénées

[THE SOUTH WEST]

[THE SOUTH WEST]

Car de l'extrême ouest jusqu'à l'extrême est, les
Pyrénées constituent une incomparable unité d'âme.
From east to west, the Pyrenees display an
incomparable unity of spirit.

Arthur Conte, French journalist and broadcaster

Bounded by the Pyrenees, the Gironde estuary
and the central plateau, south-west France is
dense in geography, history and resources.
Geography books tell us that 'the Pyrenees are
430km long and form the natural frontier
between France and Spain' - and we see a line on
the map. In truth, they are high and wide and
strong and their influence on climate and trade is
felt well north of the foothills. Their snowy caps
can be seen even in southern Gers and Pyrenean
climbing, hiking and skiing are held by
connoisseurs to be of the best.

In northern and central Aquitaine, rivers
running from the Massif Central towards the
Garonne and the Atlantic Ocean dug fertile valleys
and caves where prehistoric man found game and
shelter. He also found the inspiration for some of
humanity's first works of art, the glorious painted
caves of Lascaux. A key actor in Europe's cultural
history was already awake and the French are
proud to see their ancestry here.

The Roman civilisation rose and fell, followed in
the fifth century by the Christian Visigoths who
established a one-hundred-year kingdom stretching
from the Loire to Gibralter with Toulouse as its
capital. The city kept its importance under its feudal
counts, most called Raimond, who resisted the
authority of the king. Here was nurtured the
civilising troubadour movement whereby courtly
love and poetry became more desirable than blood
and thunder. Their language was not French but
Occitan (still spoken by some) and they cultivated
good food, literature and fine art.

In 1152, Eleanor of Aquitaine's marriage to
Henry Plantagenet put her rich province in the lap
of the English, a matter that was to take many years
and lives to resolve. By the end of the Hundred Years
War, when the French crown recovered the territory,
the English had learned to appreciate the wines of
Bordeaux, already one of the region's most
prosperous trades, and the fat Agen prune had been
'invented' by the grafting skills of the monks of
Clairac. In contrast, the coastal plains remained
deserted swamps behind their sterile dunes until the
eighteenth century. Then, pine trees were planted
to drain the swamps and stop the dunes advancing;
the Landes département is now one of France's
richest sources of timber.

Throughout the Middle Ages, thousands of
pilgrims crossed the south-west on their way to
Compostela, receiving bodily and spiritual
hospitality in Moissac, Toulouse, Cahors, Conques,
Sainte Foy and other places where we now admire
the Romanesque treasures - monasteries, churches,
hostels - built by the ministering clergy. This was
the first inkling of the region's talent for tourism
and it grew with every century. The rich resources
of the south-west, its food, beauty and mild
weather attract settlers and visitors still.

[THE SOUTH WEST]

Bay of Biscay

Etang d'Hourtin et de Carcans

Lac de Lacanau

GIRONDE

BORDEAUX 82

Ares

Andernos-les-Bains

Bassin d'Arcachon

Arcachon

Etang de Cazaux et de Sanguinet

Etang de Biscarrosse et de Parentis

Mimizan Plage

Côte d'Argent

Morcenx

LANDES

Mont-de-Marsan

Hossegor St-Vincent-de-Tyrosse St Paul les Dax

Capbreton Dax

Peyrehorade Hagetmau

BIARRITZ BAYONNE

Hendaye Bidache

PYRÉNÉES Mourenx Pau

ATLANTIQUES 86

Oloron-Ste-Marie 90

SPAIN

N

98 Bourdeilles

Ribérac

Périgueux

DORDOGNE

Lussac Ste-Foy-la-Grande

Libourne Bergerac Sarlat Souillac

94

CANTAL

Barrage de Sarran

LOT-ET-GARONNE

LOT

Tonneins Espalion

Villeneuve-sur-Lot 102 Villefranche-de-Rouergue

Agen Rodez Sévérac-le-Château

TARN-ET- AVEYRON

GARONNE Caussade Cordes-sur-Ciel

Montauban 118 Carmaux

GERS Gaillac Albi

TARN

Auch 106 Blagnac Graulhet

TOULOUSE 114

Le Mirail Castres

HAUTE- Muret Mazamet

Masseube GARONNE

HÉRAULT

Tarbes 110

Lourdes St-Gaudens

HAUTES- Pamiers

PYRÉNÉES AUDE

St-Girons Foix

Parc National ARIÈGE

des Pyrénées

ANDORRA

| 0 | 20 | 40 | 60 | 80 | 100 kilometres |

| 0 | 20 | 40 | 60 miles |

Special places to stay

Aquitaine

Midi - Pyrénées

Ecolodge des Chartrons

AQUITAINE

Looking back on their past, the people of Aquitaine are as proud of the 'influence anglaise' that shaped their culture as the English are of the Norman Conquest, although their ancestors may have tried at times to dislodge the yoke. The connection was kicked off by the dynastic marriage in 1152 of Eleanor, Duchess of Aquitaine and former Queen of France, to Henry Plantagenet, great-grandson of William the Conqueror. Henry soon managed to secure the throne of England and Aquitaine came under English rule; eventually, he reigned over lands lying between the Scottish borders and Navarre, a vast new market for the wines of the Bordeaux region.

In 1307, over a million bottles of red wine (fruity and highly alcoholic in those days) were ordered for Edward II's right royal wedding festivities. But, despite the occasional party, the Anglo-French feudal relationship went from fraught to frankly awful until the last battle of the Hundred Years War in 1453, after which the English retired to their island.

In the centuries when overland travel was slow and difficult, Bordeaux was perfectly placed for shipping local wine, in nine-hundred-litre barrels, into the Gironde estuary and up the coast to northern France and England. As a hangover from three centuries of English occupation English wine merchants ruled the export trade in the port of Bordeaux for many years, marrying into the great wine families, building warehouses along the port and grand houses in town. The northward left bank of the Garonne, however, remained a pestilential swamp until the Carthusian monks (*les Chartreux*), refugees from war-ridden Périgord, drained the area and built a new Charterhouse there in 1381.

This neighbourhood, named 'Les Chartrons' in their honour, is where Véronique found the unregenerate seventeenth-century trading house she wanted. "It was a stroke of luck," she says. "I needed raw bones – stones, timbers, iron – with nothing modernised or plastered, so as to create my dream of an upmarket eco-guesthouse from scratch. I found stone-vaulted storage spaces on the ground floor, two habitable floors above and, up a very steep staircase, some fine attics."

It's harder to be green in a city than in the country and Véronique and Yann have made every effort and done well enough to earn an Écolabel Européen. Visitors have called it "a superb place, individual and seductive, and the sitting room is a marvellous jumble, so brilliantly put together." "But the Ecolabel is not easy to live up to," says Véronique, "they are altering the criteria already, on renewable electricity, for example, and we shall have to pass the test again. For the moment, we can't consider investing in that extra level. The response from guests, though, has been interesting. Some people

"It's harder to be green in a city than in the country and Véronique and Yann have made every effort and done well enough to earn an Écolabel Européen"

actually choose our B&B because it's green; they want to know the green details, hear our tips on best practice. Others discover an attitude they had never met and we can see that it gets them thinking."

Asked where her environmental fibre comes from, she replies: "I grew up in the country and have always loved wood and stone, all natural materials in fact. I have to admit that it was easier being young then for we weren't assaulted by a million temptations to buy superfluous goods that are made to appear irresistible. There are no televisions in the rooms here. I have eaten organic food for many years, too, and it was normal that I should look for the healthy materials options when renovating the house, just as I look for healthy ingredients in food."

So she and Yann put their earth-saving principles into action, compromising neither the planet nor stylish comfort and worked non-stop for two years. They stripped the original wide floorboards – beautiful seventeenth-century Vosges pine encrusted with the dirt and varnish of ages -, uncovered the original stone well and sink, insulated with cork and wool, fitted solar panels (the first ever allowed by the authorities in the historic centre of Bordeaux), installed sun pipes to pour light into high-modern shower rooms and furnished the many rooms with family pieces and things found for Véronique by her local antique-

dealer friends, Catherine and Olivia. "They know that I like pieces with character, not necessarily grand things but pieces that carry a story. The Chesterfield sofa is remarked upon by many guests, the wrought-iron tables and chairs in the patio are full of age and personality. It's just a happy coincidence that the 'ancestor' over the mantelpiece looks very like my father." This is where she leaves a clutch of wine glasses and a corkscrew for guests who come back from vineyard tours: they often bring samples they want to taste before going out to dinner.

There's no need for a car in Bordeaux for it's on a flat flood plain and you can go everywhere by bicycle. It's a lovely ride along the embankments of the Garonne, starting with the magnificently rearing horses of the Girondins fountain, moving on to the mind-baffling mirror fountain (not to be missed), then through the public gardens and into the old neighbourhoods with their grand old houses. "We have an excellent tram system, too," says Véronique. "I only take my car when I am going outside the city."

On foot from the front door, it's just a few yards to the waterside and the rows of old warehouses that have been imaginatively converted into cafés, shops and galleries, an enchanting gateway to this exceptionally civilised, slower-than-most city.

Véronique Daudin

Ecolodge des Chartrons,
23 rue Raze, 33000 Bordeaux
- 5: 1 double, 3 twins/doubles, 1 triple.
- €110-€130.
- Restaurant 100m.
- +33 (0)5 56 81 49 13
- www.ecolodgedeschartrons.com
- Train station: Bordeaux

Clos Mirabel

AQUITAINE

André and Ann had a dream, a demanding one. They wanted, in south-west France, a vibrant year-round community that they could become part of, not one that lived by tourism alone in economic and social imbalance – hell in summer, desert in winter. They wanted a good local school for young Emily, beauty, clean air, clean land, no noise or light pollution, and a house that could be sustainably renovated. Clos Mirabel has all of that.

For two years they hunted for it. They had both worked all over the world, were living in central London and holidaying in France and Quebec. Ann, the Irish/Scots polyglot international worker, and André, the diplomat from Quebec, decided at the end of their London posting to stay in Europe. Clos Mirabel, in the royal Pyrenean province of Béarn, came up for sale in 2003 – but the photographs didn't do it justice and Ann wasn't keen. Then, in extraordinary circumstances, they went to visit the property in all its splendour and its truly remarkable setting, standing as it does among the gentle rolling hills and vineyards of Jurançon against the backdrop of the whole chain of the Atlantic Pyrenees. Whereupon André said "If this isn't it, I wonder what we could be looking for?" Ann instantly agreed. They lived here for two years to understand the house from the inside before changing anything, while caring for Ann's mother who spent her last two years at the heart of the family, drinking in the beauty of the sunsets and the ever-changing light.

After the nightmare of renovation (they planned a year, it took two), André and Ann feel they are here "as custodians, to protect, preserve and share the beauty of the place." They kept all Mirabel's historic features while installing sustainable heating systems: heat pumps, high-quality solar panels and a hugely efficient ceramic fireplace stove, made to measure in the north, that radiates massive heat from a small

wood fire. The wood supply is guaranteed for years by the thirty trees that fell in the great storm of January 2009. Guests find a bottle of warming Armagnac waiting before that fire when they return from dinner.

Breakfast the next morning, in dining room or terrace, will be a fine spread of local and organic foods. The Ossau valley, visible from the house, is where the cheese-maker lives; he stores his equipment at Mirabel and cuts their two meadows, supplying them with his superb handmade cheeses in exchange for the hay. The land is rich – and unsuitable for intensive agriculture. "Our organic eggs, unpasteurised organic milk, yogurt and butter come from local farms," says Ann, "our weekly veg basket comes from a local organic association; our fine kiwi bower gives a bumper crop each year and there are apple and pear orchards, fig and cherry trees." Some of the harvest is turned into jams and compotes for family and guests.

A real city boy, André calls himself 'an asphalt sparrow', yet he has been a keen sportsman with a thirst for the great outdoors. He has adapted happily to his new life and his knowledge of country lore grows by the year. "Keeping bees had been a mere dream. I now have three hives and my bees feed in the estate's gigantic lime, chestnut and acacia trees, giving quantities of fine-scented honey; I am loving it." The trees flower at different periods so he can harvest the spare honey of one flowering before the next is garnered. He and Ann are learning vegetable gardening. "We've chosen the easy options first – tomatoes, pumpkins, courgettes. The ruined potager was huge once, half a hectare, and the old watering system is still there. We'd love to get it all going again." Under the courtyard lies a vast tank harvesting rainwater from the roofs for use in the house, the gardens, the swimming pool and the fishpond.

Before returning to Tahiti, the former owner introduced Ann, André and Emily to his circle of friends who had all loved coming to Clos Mirabel. They instantly adopted the new family and acted as guides to the traditions that mark the local calendar such as making pâtés and sausages, still common down here, gathering mushrooms, harvesting soft fruit, curing

salmon from the river at Navarranx. The Pélonquin-Kennys' Scottish, Irish and Québecois origins have equipped them with a good dose of natural hospitality; the people of the Béarn have the same fibre and the village is a vital ingredient in their new lives. Apart from sitting on the council of Emily's school, they are part of a new environment protection group in Jurançon that promotes renewable energy and conservation and aims to convince the local population of the enduring value of this attitude.

This is the story so far, but it is part of an ongoing project to create a small seminar centre and health spa here. Plans have been drawn up by Giovanna Anselmi, their Italian architect who specialises in renovation and sustainable architecture, sensitively blending new with old as she does in Rome.

Deeply fulfilled in their new life, Ann and André "revel daily in the extraordinary views of the Pyrenees, a majestic presence as far as the eye can see, a true gift of nature."

Ann Kenny & André Péloquin

Clos Mirabel,
276 av. des Frères Barthélémy, 64110 Jurançon
- 2 + 3: 2 doubles. 1 apt for 4. 2 gîtes, each for 6.
- €95-€120. Extra person €35.
- Restaurants 3km.
- +33 (0)5 59 06 32 83
- www.closmirabel.com
- Train station: Pau

Maison Rancèsamy

AQUITAINE

In French folk history the old province of Béarn is the cradle of *le Bon Roi Henri IV*, the popular seventeenth-century monarch who renounced his Protestant upbringing to become king of this Catholic country and declared that he would "put a boiled hen on every table every week". Unrealistic, of course, but his generous spirit lingers here and Isabelle speaks of "a strong community of open-minded, genuine people. Unrushed and interested, they talk to each other across the generations."

In 1995, the Brownes chose to leave South Africa, Simon's fruit farm, their farm school, and Isabelle's art gallery, to be nearer their families in Europe. The move involved a leap of faith – and sixteen days at sea, as Simon and Isabelle thought it important for their young children not to make the 8,000-kilometre change overnight.

Why France? Isabelle, with her French and Polish origins, loved France, and Simon is "a true republican and wanted a country without a crown." As he discovered, France may no longer have a crown but it has many coronets and an enduringly elitist social system. "If you haven't read Balzac and Zola you can't understand contemporary France. Nothing has changed; there's loads of sucking up to old Bourbons – just look at the obituaries." A "gentle giant, larger than life", as Isabelle says of him, he is calmly indignant as he gets on with his plan to extract himself from the clutches of commerce and banking. "Until plastic cards are as free as cheques, we cannot accept them. Our small business resists the banking onslaught that fuels a world of consumer spending and inflation, the things that devalue hard-earned cash."

Why the Béarn? It is one of the least spoilt regions of France. Its remoteness behind the swamps of the Landes kept it free of invaders and generations of pastoral farmers have lived here in peace, far from

the sound of sabres or cannons, with a profound sense of belonging. Its lush rolling hills and the majestic Pyrenees are home to ancient forests of acacia, chestnut, oak and wild cherry. Walking is magical, where endless rivers – called *gaves* – gush down the mountainsides. With sure instinct, Simon will recommend secret backways with breathtaking views and the best eateries. "There are boar, deer and badgers out there and twice a year," says Isabelle, "squadrons of migrating cranes fly over and thrill the listener with their plaintive cry, an ephemeral treat for those who are out of doors and taking notice." She also delights in sitting still, waiting for the great variety of frogs and birds to show their shy selves.

Isabelle visits other gardens to gather insider tips for the 'home farm' ("what do you use instead of foul-smelling macerated nettle to repel bugs?") while Simon plants and patches and prunes in the big garden, producing ever greater quantities of flowers, fruit and vegetables. Isabelle then turns them into delicious dishes – she loves doing vegetarian food – and jams and compotes for her gourmet meals. Simon's conversations with neighbours often turn on the relative merits of chicken, cow or donkey manure. "In the Cape, people boiled tobacco leaves against pests but I need to find a fixer here to hold the stuff on the leaves in our heavy mountain rain. In winter, I lay plastic sheeting to suffocate the weeds, then I whip it off in spring and the ground is perfect: no weeds and not too damp." He is making plans for chickens and sheep, too, but "you have to have a banker if you want cows."

Nothing much is thrown away here. The inlaid chestnut tables are old barn doors and the wood for the stoves comes from trees that have fallen on their land. Isabelle, yoga addict and former art-gallery owner, has made their lovely house into something of a showcase for things collected on their travels: carvings, paintings and pots by many artist friends. Her new life running a B&B takes her away from her drawing pad but brings her closer to people. She is a member of Slow Food and sources almost everything from home or nearby. "Our four markets carry ultra-

local rarities such as 'oignons de Trébons' and 'greuil' (fresh ewe's-milk curds), and I so enjoy the guests' astonishment when they ask for herb tea and see me reaching into the garden, even in the dark, to pluck a sprig of lemon balm or verbena or thyme."

The gathering in the courtyard at the end of the day is an opportunity for the Brownes to explain why they have chosen this neo-rural way of life and

> "Simon plants and patches and prunes in the big garden, producing ever greater quantities of flowers, fruit and vegetables. Isabelle then turns them into delicious dishes"

why they consider it vitally important for the future of the planet. Then it's time for dinner, where freshly-gathered garden produce, transformed into fine, artistically-presented food, comes to the beautiful big table. There may be a bottle of the famous local Jurançon wine, or a rare 'brebis d'estive' artisan cheese, made in pure traditional fashion by the shepherds while their sheep graze the fragrant high mountain pastures during the summer months.

And to make the evening perfect, the Bechstein grand piano, a family heirloom, is there for the playing.

Simon & Isabelle Browne

Maison Rancèsamy,
Quartier Rey, 64290 Lasseube
- 5: 2 doubles, 1 twin, 2 family rooms.
- €75-€90. Family room €108-€125.
- Dinner with wine, €32.
- +33 (0)5 59 04 26 37
- www.missbrowne.com
- Train station: Pau

Château des Baudry

AQUITAINE

"Ours is a noble château", says François, "but it's not a grand one set about with flourishes and turrets". No, it is definitely on the domestic side of château-ness, an idiosyncratic country house with a rough, strong face surveying miles of lush landscape. The group of thickset buildings stands four-square round the most seductive lily-pond courtyard – shades of a Roman villa? a cloister? – and carries a lot of history.

For three hundred years the home of Protestant squires, Les Baudry has a sense of great age and enduring shelter. Gazing out over the countryside, you can almost feel its eyes looking down its long aristocratic nose.

When Louis XIII gave the influential Pauvert de la Chapelle family aristocratic status early in the seventeenth century, they extended the simple two-hundred-year-old farmhouse they were living in. A few decades later, they adopted the new ideas of social economy propounded by the Physiocratic School (government by nature) inspired by Montesquieu and Diderot, ideas that announced Adam Smith's economic principles to be laid down in 1776. Keen to develop the estate and bring prosperity to willing, well-treated workers, the Pauverts built their model farm here in 1768.

A century later, all the farm's activities were gathered together in three new buildings, creating a surprisingly Italianate enclosed space, most unusual in the south-west. Grand reception rooms were decorated with fine panelling and carved fireplaces, life became more elegant, though still soberly Protestant, and the dead were buried among their own in the little family cemetery.

The next owners were even more original. When the Pauverts died out in the 1940s, the house was bought by dairy farmers from Normandy. They came with their tan-and-white cows, pulled up the vines, planted hedges and apple trees – and created a little

piece of Normandy on this Périgordian hilltop. They bravely produced milk and cream without an iota of modern equipment, tilling the land with horses, milking the cows by hand in the fields, until they too died out in 2006, leaving the house as they had found it sixty years earlier.

Just as the land had never been subjected to aggressive fertilisers, weedkillers or pesticides, the buildings had never been altered by modern plumbing, heating or wiring. François and Hélène arrived with reforming zeal, changed the destiny of Les Baudry from farming to tourism and brought it all into the twenty-first century – with huge respect for its history and Calvinist purity. The works revealed long-hidden marvels such as the two dressed-stone doorways that are over five hundred years old. In the younger parts, "the style is utterly Protestant, refined, simple and sober: look how they built to the human scale, how they laid their tiles to enhance the perspectives!" After three years of non-stop renovation, including careful painting of the noble 'French' ceilings, they find Les Baudry has worked its way into their sinews; they know and love every detail and have furnished it with their antiques (they are zealous hunter-gatherers) and a light hand. "The eye is at rest at all times," is one visitor's comment.

Hélène cooks in the same spirit of simplicity and goodness, gathering her ingredients from local markets: "there's one almost every day within ten kilometres of us and Sainte Foy la Grande is listed as one of the most beautiful markets in France. I never go to a supermarket." The potager, where things grow willingly in untainted soil, produces volumes of summer fruits and the herbs Hélène so delights in using. Her 'aubergines aux herbes' is worth the detour, as Michelin would say. She says she's incapable of cooking and sitting with guests at the same time. "In any case, we find that guests, especially French guests, are happier at separate tables, though of course people do get friendly in this lovely place, in which case they ask to share a table. We love it when this happens."

Having come from making a huge success of a much larger place, she enjoys being closer to her guests and having more time for them, and she finds

that the lovely patio garden and its trickling, lilting pond, the heart of the house, brings them quietly together. "There are no televisions in the rooms and contemplation comes naturally. The total silence of the place has a cleansing effect."

"Our Dordogne is not High-Street Dordogneshire," adds François, "it's a place where guests come to be among French people and we take our time to do things for them. Our advice is tailormade to each guest." There are vineyards of all shapes and sizes to visit; François and Hélène know the best ones well. "We are on the border between Dordogne and St Émilion and, most unusually, 50% of the wine-growers of the Saussignac area are organic." Which suits the ethos of Les Baudry.

Meanwhile, the newly-planted hornbeam hedges prosper, the fruit bushes deliver generously, the three big friendly dogs sniff the breeze and half a dozen eventing ponies, mares and their young, graze the days away until they go to the training centre.

Hélène Boulet & François Passebon

Château des Baudry,
24240 Monestier
- 4: 1 double, 3 twins/doubles.
- €120-€150.
- Breakfast €12. Dinner €32. Wine €12-€32.
- +33 (0)5 53 23 46 42
- www.chateaudesbaudry.com
- Train station: Ste Foy la Grande

Pauliac

AQUITAINE

"We were really young and working in England – John a history teacher, I a librarian – with no great career plans," says Jane. "One day, my father announced he was planning to do B&B in his house in Dordogne – but he went to Saudi Arabia instead." So they decided to leave their jobs, buy the house next door to his and try it themselves for a couple of years. "The children were young enough to adapt..." That was twenty years ago. They are still enjoying it wholeheartedly, constantly discovering new things about the language and culture of their adopted country.

They had both changed countries before, to and from South Africa, and knew they loved wide-open countryside and home-grown food. So they slid lightly into Pauliac, two stone farmhouses in a self-sufficient hamlet of six, and their hectare of land. Their predecessor had kept pigs in the old stone sheds beside the farm's huge water tank. Unusually, the tank faces south, a stroke of luck this : "it was asking to be turned into a delightful, secluded plunge-pool surrounded by original outhouses of great character."

Character is everywhere here. John and Jane built the lower pool themselves (waist deep, it's ideal for children); the water cascades from the one to the other through a spout in the wall like a great shower and, finished with yellow

oxide paint, the pools look like natural ponds.

Jane started life as a city librarian and enjoyed it, but she is totally fulfilled now, living in deepest Dordogne and cooking every single evening. "I just love cooking, and teaching others to cook. Food is our priority here and it takes time; my courses teach people the value of taking proper time in the kitchen and I encourage them to make their own pastry and mayonnaise. Many of my recipes are traditional and use cuts of meat that require slow cooking rather than twice-kissed steak, for example."

The kitchen garden gives lettuces, tomatoes, courgettes and herbs, there are apples, plums, walnuts, hazelnuts and quince on the trees. Jane's quince jelly goes wonderfully with cheese from the nearby organic goat farm and she gets her meat from an old family butcher. Organic bread and cheeses are local, too. "Our brocanteur friend has broad beans galore, and tomatoes and courgettes when ours rot or run out. The nearby 'magasin universel', the Harrods of the Dordogne, sells masses of organic stuff as well as refrigerators."

Evenings are important at Pauliac. Jane describes the form: "No-one rushes off to a restaurant. I feed the children early while the adults change, then we spend all

evening over dinner. The food comes in little by little, punctuating convivial conversation." They do lots of groups – writing, painting or cookery courses – and get to know people really well, reducing guests' eco-footprints at the same time.

"The house isn't grand but I hope people can find sparks of inspiration in the decoration. I enjoy redoing something each winter. I like to

"No-one rushes off to a restaurant. I feed the children early while the adults change, then we spend all evening over dinner. The food comes in little by little, punctuating convivial conversation"

dramatic or surprising look for the least expense as I'll want to rearrange things again soon enough. I do everything – except the roof of this very high house." Built on the side of a hill overlooking the valley below, the house 'walks' down the slope, changing levels with a quirky gait. The big salon, however, has a serious past: it was the school for children from all the surrounding villages.

John's great love is the enchanting hillside garden that he has made from nothing, starting at the little old farmyard that already had three mature shady trees. You come up the narrow sombre lane and suddenly it opens onto glory. The upper terraces are a festival of flowers and shrubby corners for sitting. "I love plants and exuberance," he says, "I don't plan colour coordinations, I just make a few concessions to height, but it only needs a little tinkering now (that includes weeding by hand) and never a drop of chemical anything." The soil is not very good, just ten centimetres on top of the limestone, "and local farmers growing industrial maize and sunflowers are realising how they've botched things up by removing copses and

hedgerows. The last five years have brought more big storms than ever before and terrible erosion. But roses like it; luckily, our dogs, Pilot the old labrador and Dan the enthusiastic young bouvier, keep the rose-greedy deer at bay." There are two great cats, too, characters both.

The natural simplicity of their welcome and the sureness of their taste make John and Jane the easiest people to be with. As John puts it: "We love living here and don't plan to go anywhere else. Life is Slow, varied, even quite exciting, in a gentle way. Summer is fairly intense, winter is more restful with a new project or two (this year I'm building new dining tables so we can be more flexible); we have a mix of friends and we take our time over everything. I'm very slow on the tennis court, too."

Jane & John Edwards

Pauliac,
Celles, 24600 Ribérac
- 4: 2 doubles, 1 twin, 1 suite for 4.
- €65.
- Dinner €25. Wine €10.
- +33 (0)5 47 23 40 17
- www.pauliac.fr
- Train station: Périgueux

Château de Rodié

AQUITAINE

Trees, plants, animals and humans thrive in this region of hills and thick-grown valleys that is quintessential south-west France. Prehistoric men knew it and settled in the sheltering caves, developing their social and hunting skills and leaving their spiritual legacy of men and beasts, bows and arrows, on the walls.

Meeting in the twentieth century, Paul and Pippa found they shared a love of nature and rural life and a fascination for old buildings, coupled to an overriding concern about the dangers of unsustainable consumerism. To fulfil their ideals, they wanted to work from home, so they bought a derelict medieval fortress on a wooded hillside with fifty-six hectares. The property had been used as farm buildings since the French Revolution and the land left overgrown or intensively grazed.

"It's a gem," Paul says, "a marvel, the fortress of every boy's dreams on a human scale." During the seven years of restoration ("there's plenty more to do") they have found many traces of its history: Roman tiles, coins, buckles, a medieval saquebut (a hooked lance for pulling enemies off battlements). "The origins of Rodié are lost in the fog of time but every angle was covered by artillery, first rocks, then gunpowder." The two hundred years of dereliction meant there were no recent renovations to undo and they could "set about the château's resurrection from a clean slate, to create a haven of calm for people, plants and animals."

When we asked the Hecquets "Are you really green?" Paul quipped: "Not green, heliotrope!" The reasons for such eco-commitment would fill a small book but one is instantly struck by how deeply he and Pippa care. "But there's no preaching here, ever," says Pippa. "we just hope people will see and appreciate what we do and why." One of the more 'shocking' things they did was not repointing the

building so the thick limestone walls are home to myriads of small beasts and plants.

Having rebuilt the castle using timber and stone from their valley and materials recovered from necessary demolition, they decorated it 'en famille' with chalk and lime mixes, furnished it with antiques

> "It's a gem," Paul says, "a marvel, the fortress of every boy's dreams on a human scale"

(aka recycled furniture), and decided to home-school their two small daughters (now fifteen and thirteen); that includes, of course, natural sciences and organic farming, by osmosis. Apart from comfortable guest quarters, they run an organic farm. This keeps them pretty busy. All the family is involved in the farm and the girls love going up the hill with Paul and the four dogs every evening on 'lamb patrol' to check that the fences and sheep are in order. The views from the plâteau are heart-stopping and on a clear day you can see the Pyrenees.

Rare breeds of sheep and goats were chosen to help return the land to proper rural balance after years of disuse, and it shows. The Hecquets are part of an old-breed seed bank producing hardy seed stock that's adapted to the local environment, can be replanted and has not been hybridised for commerce. They produce all the poultry, eggs, lamb and most fruit and veg needed for the guests and themselves, the rest coming from local or organic suppliers where possible. One of Pippa's great interests is old-style cooking and recipes. "We specialise in food which is sadly getting rarer," she says, "classic country cooking such as poule au pot, coq au vin, 'agneau à l'agenaise' (lamb with prunes) and 'the oldest stew of all': throw in all you've got, add lots of wine and herbs and simmer." Americans are amazed to see this done in an iron pot over an open fire and overjoyed to share it in the immense Great Hall. Pippa commands a formidable battery of equipment, some new ("the French army recently downsized their kitchens and we have some

of the most fearsome engines of culinary war you could imagine") and some extremely old, including a fifteenth-century oil jar "not for daily use". She harvests oyster mushrooms in season and is constantly on the lookout for new and unusual vegetables. "Don't worry," she says, "I test them on the family first. A neolithic stew never caught on with Paul and the girls so we haven't tried it on the guests!"

Paul works the land with restored old farm equipment, including a 53-year-old Massey Ferguson. The family Landrover runs on a converted tractor engine and they practise hyper-miling (squeezing the maximum number of miles out of a gallon of fuel). "I defy even a Prius owner to prove they leave a smaller ecological footprint; a Landrover never dies." Their other one is twenty years old and has done 750,000 km with no engine change.

The family have formidable energy. They have recently installed a giant wood-fired boiler, baptised Hades, to heat practically half the castle. The next project is to harness a spring down through a stepped series of forty 1000-litre tanks (recovered wine vats) to create enough pressure to supply all their domestic water needs and "relieve the water company's burden."

"Rodié is a way of life and, whatever the highly-strung urbanite may think, this is the real world. Try dealing with a sheep's prolapse at two in the morning or reconstructing a collapsed twelfth-century rampart by popping down to your local DIY! The love that most of our guests have for Rodié is humbling and if one or two pause for thought when they're next in the megastore, then it's all worthwhile."

Paul & Pippa Hecquet

Château de Rodié,
47370 Courbiac de Tournon
* 5: 4 doubles, 1 suite.
* €78-€110.
* Dinner with wine, €20.
* +33 (0)5 53 40 89 24
* www.chateauderodie.com
* Train station: Agen or Cahors

Domaine de Peyloubère

MIDI - PYRÉNÉES

Watered by many rivers and romantic memories of favourite sons d'Artagnan, the fourth of the Three Musketeers, and Cyrano de Bergerac (both real people), Gascony is a life-nurturing land and the Gers is its remote, rural and authentically French heart. Through the centuries, the people of Gascony have borne a reputation for hotheadedness and obstinacy, yet Theresa has always found them "kind, patient and delightful, the opposite of the city types we lived with before, who appeared to be driven by status and money alone. In Auch, our capital, even the most harassed bureaucrats take a leisurely lunch break."

When she and Ian arrived in Pavie twelve years ago, they heard farmers saying "Yes, my son's taking over the farm"; they saw families of cows, including the bull, grazing together in the fields; they watched locals playing slow reflective pétanque in the soft evening sun; they learned about the 'quart d'heure gersois' which forgives a fifteen-minute late arrival;

and they were converted to this sense of slow continuity. The thirty-five-hectare estate of Peyloubère needed massive amounts of work and they thought "Yes, we too would like to improve it then pass it on."

After years of hard slog on land and buildings, they feel they are caretaking their piece of the country as much for the community as for their family and guests. They work with the walking club to maintain the footpaths that criss-cross the estate, which includes a stretch of the River Gers, and provide a meandering riverside route into the village for cottage guests to collect breakfast croissants. In the same spirit, the Martins supported the reintroduction of the weekly market in Pavie, ensuring an outlet for thirteen organic farmers in the commune and beyond.

Leaving London and demanding lives, convinced that education is the basis for change, they planned to start a languages centre in the hamlet. But there was

so much to be done at home, in chalk, brambles, dust and mud, that they plunged into the earthy and left the cerebral behind. Helping them in spirit was the legacy of Mario Cavaglieri, the Italian painter who lived, loved (his muse, model and later wife) and painted here for over forty years in the middle of the last century. Not only did he record the people, terraces and gardens of Peyloubère on canvas, he imprinted his own history and passions on the house itself. The ceilings, walls and cupboards of the Manoir are alive with uncerebral bodies, colours and imaginative ideas, now enjoyed by lucky B&B guests. Cavaglieri also laid out the beautiful Italian gardens.

But there's nothing prissy or delicate. Ian and Theresa agree that "it's wonderful when urban kids make dens in hedges, when those who were afraid of ants end up gathering tadpoles from the lake. We see them arrive with teeth-gritting, paranoid dad; before two days are out, he doesn't care what the children get up to: in the good solid house they've rented, there's no fear of damage. We have young parents from towns who come to enjoy their children and the beautiful quiet countryside. This is what Peyloubère is for."

"I love cooking for small mixed groups, things like homemade pâté and home-grown veg, nothing flashy, just fresh, good and convivial." Both Ian and Theresa are absorbed at Peyloubère, starting with breakfast, when B&B guests want them to be there. Then the rooms need doing. "Then," says Theresa, "I may take a trip to feed the ducklings and spend an hour duck gazing. Ian and I protect our lunchtime together, it's the moment in the day when we can talk, relax, even play a game over coffee. And plan our future... Will it be painting courses? or music? or yoga? There's an inspirational yoga teacher on the other side of Auch..."

Their loyal gardener, Kader, arrives after lunch. "He's been with us for ten years and still can't get the idea that Monsanto are banned. On the open day (Journées du Patrimoine), he was showing people round as if the whole place was his, he loves Peyloubère but, like all French individuals, he has his idiosyncrasies – such as putting weedkiller on the drive when we're not looking." Unless there's shopping to do or they take a rare walk, they both spend the afternoon in the potager with Kader. It's a highly successful no-dig no-chemicals garden, with the hens nearby in the old hunting dogs' pen.

"It's a real pleasure to see our guests unwind and enjoy the simple things: the taste of fresh market produce, eggs from our hens or veg from our garden; to wonder at the kingfisher darting over lake or waterfall, the perfection of the bee orchid hidden in the long grass. Living through the seasons here is a privilege: watering from the river in summer, pruning in the autumn and seeing the shape of things to come, waiting through the winter then watching it all unfold again."

And Theresa concludes: "When guests turn in through the old gates and reach the circular rose garden in front of the mellow ivied walls of the Manoir, we can feel their relief as the relaxed bohemian atmosphere of Peyloubère starts its healing process."

Theresa & Ian Martin

Domaine de Peyloubère,
32550 Pavie
- 2 suites.
- €90-€110.
- Dinner with wine, €30.
- +33 (0)5 62 05 74 97
- www.peyloubere.com
- Train station: Auch

Gratia

MIDI - PYRÉNÉES

This is beautiful, secret Ariège, a land of gentle curves and sudden hills, clear streams and few people, where the flatness of the Toulouse plain becomes more shapely before coming up against the sharp sheer Pyrenees.

History has swept over the region like the wild mountain winds. Each impregnable hill was topped by a stronghold, defended by a succession of kings, counts and invaders. The best-known conflict must be the tragedy of the so-called Albigensian heresy, a bitter mix of religion and politics that ended in the massacre of thousands of white-robed Cathars. Their aim was to become 'perfect' and they believed, pacifically, in the Manichean credo of two separate spiritual forces, one good, one evil, rather than a single all-encompassing God. Rome could not countenance the dogma and launched what was called a Christian Crusade, a devastating Holy War conducted by 'the church's eldest daughter', France, and her barons of the north, Simon de Montfort in the lead, against the peace-loving 'heretics' of the south.

Lézat lies slightly north of these blood-soaked memories. Peaceful beneath its plane trees, the village square is essential rural France, an invitation to change gear, slow

down and adopt the pace of a gentle game of boules with the locals. Then lunch at the café, perhaps, and a twenty-minute walk back across the lovely rolling hillside that leads up to Gratia through countryside that has inspired the local nickname of 'little Tuscany'. It is a hikers' paradise: hikes go from not-too-strenuous to highly-demanding and well-informed walkers, cyclists, climbers and skiers try to keep the county's unsung glories close to their chests. Others come for the wealth of medieval castles, villages and churches.

A shaded track leads through Gratia's woodland and bursts into sunlight at the end. When Florence and Jean-Paul first visited the property, they came down this track to a total ruin where wild horses were living. In their fifties, they were looking for an alternative to their highly-strung northern-city life, "a place where our lives would be more authentic, more in harmony with nature." They fell for the quiet architectural elegance of Gratia and its genuine old stones, its woods and fields full of birds, hares and deer.

The work required was awe-inspiring but they were spurred on by the beauty of the impressive timbers and original fireplace. To their delight, they discovered hidden treasure in the attic: a stock of untouched original floor tiles. Jean-Paul's motto of "less is more" and Florence's talent have governed the whole process. It is stunningly, simply elegant, full of original or recycled materials used with eco-flair and attention to detail. Any hint of a designer touch is deflected by a sideways sense of humour such as the blue-glass bottles in the bathroom – arranged on the floor under the basin.

The long low farmhouse was built in the 1790s in three parts, one end for cows, the other for sheep, the middle for people – a comfortable house for prosperous farmers in the pure local pale-brick style that settles gently into the landscape. Two thirds of the upper floor are now one vast space where Florence paints and gives massage and relaxation treatments and where they both listen to music. "I like classical best," she says, "and Bach's my favourite." "And I like soul best," says Jean-Paul – an intriguing combination. Their tastes reflect their personalities, one clearcut and ordered, the other 'cooler' with a discreet passion or two. Florence admits that "people are different in the south, they

> "The work required was awe-inspiring but they were spurred on by the beauty of the impressive timbers and original fireplace"

live out of doors and don't open their houses so spontaneously, just meeting in the street or at the café. They are less punctual, too; we have had to soften the edges of our characters a bit! But not for a second have we regretted our move."

They garden together, in shrubberies and borders, orchard and potager; water comes from the well, the surrounding fields are the perfect foil, as neatly

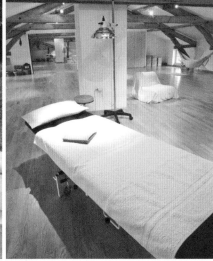

manicured as the lawns of Gratia. "We live with the seasons and have learned that working the earth with your hands is a powerful way to recharge your energies."

Jean-Paul devotes his mornings to his other passion, the economy and the money markets. "I need to stay in touch with the world, I don't want to be cut off from contemporary society just because I don't live in a town any more," and he retreats to his study until lunchtime. This is when Florence makes her all-organic breakfast goodies for the next day – homemade cakes, raisin bread, crème caramel, and more. Breakfast is worth lingering over: Florence's myriad jams, eggs from her hens, a young, creamy local goat's cheese – they are all part of it.

The living room, another generous expanse of civilised comfort, has a great old fireplace that is fed all winter with the wood that Jean-Paul and Florence harvest together every autumn. They are still bringing in the oaks and acacias toppled by the monster gale of 1999. "We love this hard, hands-on work in the woods, and the clearing does so much good to the healthy trees. It's pleasing, too, that we can heat most of the house with our own fuel."

In a nutshell, they feel they "are protecting a little piece of the planet: the architectural heritage, the orchard with its old varieties, the brilliantly-restored potager fed by horse manure only, the land kept clean of chemicals."

Florence Potey & Jean-Paul Wallaert

Gratia,
09210 Lézat sur Lèze
- 4 doubles.
- €90-€120.
- Restaurants nearby.
- +33 (0)5 61 68 64 47
- www.ariege.com/gratia
- Train station: Toulouse

Hôtel Cuq en Terrasses

MIDI - PYRÉNÉES

These two are lovely, kind, super-sociable, brimming with talent and taste – and the after-dinner singing is a masterstroke.

Theirs is another tale of love at first sight. Philippe and Andonis were living in Paris during the week, both in high-flying corporate jobs that were losing their lustre, and filling their country house with friends at weekends when, ten years ago, they came here for a wedding and fell totally in love with the mellow old house on the hill and its surroundings. "The fields and the hills somehow create a sense of eternity" says Philippe. After six months of wrangle, the house and its twelve terraced hectares were theirs.

Both had grown up, Philippe in rural France, Andonis on a Greek island, in families for whom the Slow Food philosophy was a given: the glue of society is convivial eating and proper food needs love and respect, time to choose, time to prepare, time to share. They practised the credo so diligently that one year they realised they had only been alone for two weekends out of fifty-two. Now they have guests seven days a week, seven months a year, and revel in it. Meanwhile, Noémie, their beloved griffon, has her own canine social circle whose members have their own routines and regularly drop in on each other.

Built on the ramparts of the hilltop castle (Cuq Toulza name means 'the top of the hill on the way to Toulouse' in Occitan), the eighteenth-century presbytery had been used as the village shop, post office and bakery in the days when the hamlet had fifty inhabitants. Now there are just eleven souls, the shop has closed, the town hall has moved to the village at the bottom of the hill, and the town council comes back up the hill to dine at the 'new' gourmet restaurant.

Andonis and Philippe each brought their collections. Philippe's antiques (he started collecting

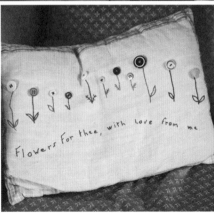

Flowers for thee, with love from me

at eleven) and paintings, which are all over the house, Andonis' two hundred copper cake moulds and even more cookery books, which are all in the kitchen. They both love people, food and travelling, to which Philippe adds "decorating and antiques" and Andonis "music and singing."

They renovated the house with loving care, a sustainability target, old timbers and tiles and subtle taste. Add contemporary art by local painters, potters and sculptors – Philippe has a fine eye for these things – and you have a house worth visiting over and over again. Heat pumps were installed for the hot water, salted pool water, and central heating; rainwater is collected in a well and the compost heap feeds the old local varieties of the ancient orchard and the new organic kitchen garden, where almost all their fruits, herbs and vegetables grow. The soil and air are so clean that orchids thrive, along with four hundred other sorts of plant, sharing the glorious seven-terraced garden with birds, rabbits, squirrels and hedgehogs. "We are conscious of the rhythms of nature: every moment and every detail needs our attention if we want to achieve those special little taste experiences we aim for, such as mousse of wood-smoked beetroot."

Cuq en Terrasses is a vegetarian's dream. Andonis' island home had no cattle on it so he grew up with his mother's fabulous fish and veg dishes and his inventivity seems to know no bounds, except those of delicousness. Together, he and Philippe make practically everything they put on the table, from breakfast cereals to all the dinner dishes and, they specify, "we make them with love and delight." Philippe loves choosing and recommending the wines. They pay the same attention to their guests, spotting the like-minded and putting them close to each other: "it generally works a treat."

At the end of dinner comes the masterstroke. Andonis appears in his chef's gear and launches the evening's slow, old-fashioned entertainment, to the occasional consternation of the unwarned guest. Philippe hands out songbooks (Cole Porter, Rodgers &

Hammerstein) while Andonis sits down at the pianola and starts pedalling. One roll follows another and by the end of the evening the shrinking violets and old sticks who had sworn they would never ever singalong with anyone will be part of the special magic that these two conjure up, making "My Way" followed by "New York, New York" irresistible. "This way of life suits us perfectly," they say in unison – and it shows.

The next day, they will advise you to avoid the Disneyland that is Carcassonne and go to harmonious, unspoilt Albi (parking is easy), to visit the remarkable brick cathedral and the Toulouse-Lautrec museum. For nature-lovers, there are a week of walks from the front door and a wonderful waterfall which isn't in the guidebooks and where one can often be alone.

Slow and special it most certainly is, and human and beautiful, too.

Philippe Gallice & Andonis Vassalos

Hôtel Cuq en Terrasses,
Cuq le Château, 81470 Cuq Toulza

- 7: 3 doubles, 3 twins/doubles, 1 suite.
- €95-€150. Suite €190. Half-board €185-€274 for 2.
- Breakfast €14. Hosted dinner €35. Wine €14-€25.
- +33 (0)5 63 82 54 00
- www.cuqenterrasses.com
- Train station: Toulouse

Château de Mayragues

MIDI - PYRÉNÉES

"Light-coloured limestone that sparkles in the sun" is how Laurence describes Mayragues. Thirty years ago, she and Alan fell for this special and unusual sparkle and bought the place despite its ruinous state. It had elementary plumbing and thirteen hectares of vines, fifty-five more hectares of pastures and woods, two listed buildings – the strong-looking sheer-walled medieval château and its captivating seventeenth-century Languedocian dovecote – and buckets of atmosphere. "And we love it still, though it's hard work. Our only burden is bureaucratic torture and red tape."

Laurence left her job as curator at the Musée Carnavalet in Paris and volunteer at the V&A in London and started on the long haul of restoration, closely supervised by the official Architect of French listed buildings. Only natural, noble, healthy materials such as hemp, local sand, lime and cork were permitted. To fund the restoration, Alan continued his job in the oil industry that took him all over the world and back home whenever he could, and always for the grape harvest. When their two children were born, Alan the wandering Scot could eventually come to live full-time at Mayragues and give all his energies to the vineyard and the art of making wine.

Wine-growing started in the Gaillac area under Roman occupation. Mayragues' vineyards are old with vines mentioned in a deed of purchase dated 1609. The oldest written record found to date goes back to 1453 and Alan found fragments of ceramic wine vessels from the second century BC at Mayragues when he was planting some new vines. The vineyards had been wholly modernised by twentieth-century wine growers to produce quantity rather than quality, including banal hybrids rather than authentic varieties. So Alan and Laurence undertook a complete restructuring

of their vineyards, grubbing up the hybrids and planting local varieties, Duras and Braucol in red, Loin de l'Oeil and Mauzac in white, to produce distinctive wines with clear personality and vigour.

Ten years later, they embarked on the adventure of converting their whole wine business to bio-dynamic methods. Alan is a persuasive convert: "Tilling the soil opens it to cosmic influences and a healthy soil encourages the vines to put down

It had elementary plumbing, thirteen hectares of vines... two listed buildings... and buckets of atmosphere

deep roots that feed the grapes on the natural elements of the *terroir**. In a conventional vineyard, the roots remain on the surface waiting to be fed with artificial fertilisers. Weedkillers, pesticides and fungicides containing synthetic chemicals have been replaced by completely natural bio-dynamic preparations used in homeopathic doses and

applied in accordance with a bio-dynamic calendar. Now, we have a controlled collection of grasses, 'weeds' and wild flowers growing between the vines, including orchids in spring (there are one hundred varieties of wild orchid in the Tarn), we have many more birds, and the wines have developed an even more typical taste of *terroir**."

The commitment to a totally natural process has brought several awards, including the precious Silver Amphora for organic wines and their very first order from a New York restaurateur (despatched in 2009). "The Slow approach is colouring our lifestyle more and more. Working with bio-dynamics ties us closely to the rhythms of nature – the moon, the seasons, the sunrise and sunset – and we find the idea of caring for plants by caring for the the earth is really beautiful. Not having television protects us from the hurly-burly of contemporary life, too."

Having taken their thirty-five hectares of farmland back from the 'conventional' tenant farmers, they have started to convert them to bio-dynamics. The plan is for crops such as hemp to alternate with animals – "we already have two donkeys!" – and help the land find its natural

balance again. The budding potager provides the raw materials for Laurence's array of breakfast jams to go with her homemade bread and home-laid eggs. They also grow walnuts and apples, and dessert grapes of course.

The château's fourteenth-century fortified architecture is typical of the region but the overhanging sentinel's gallery that softens the spartan look of the façade is one of only a few surviving examples of its kind. Outdoor concerts of chamber music and occasional theatrical performances are given beneath that façade every summer, magical candlelit affairs that marry solid old architecture to ephemeral stage art. Later that night, you will take the gallery to reach the big half-timbered B&B rooms and the wide-open views of magnificent countryside the next morning. Or you may have rented the prettiest cottage imaginable, the château's converted bakery that looks out to that fairytale dovecote where homemade swings hang invitingly between the pillars.

Mayragues is on the edge of the lovely Forêt de Grésigne where the last examples of a vanishing species of fritillary can be found among the ancient oaks. Eagles and nightingales thrill watcher and hearer, buzzards and hoopoes swing through the unpolluted air. Laurence and Alan are grateful to be contributing to the preservation of so magnificent a part of the world and they love sharing it with visitors, but you won't be bombarded with organic sermons, just left to enjoy the benefits.

* Terroir - see notes on p. 242

Laurence & Alan Geddes

Château de Mayragues,
81140 Castelnau de Montmiral
• 2: 1 double, 1 twin. Min. stay 2 nights. Cottage for 3.
• €85-€90. Cottage €400-€500 per week.
• Restaurants within 4km.
• +33 (0)5 63 33 94 08
• www.chateau-de-mayragues.com
• Train station: Gaillac

Auvergne   Rhône Valley - Alps

[AUVERGNE]

[AUVERGNE]

Ce n'est pas la Suisse, c'est plus terrible, ce n'est pas l'Italie, c'est plus beau, c'est la France centrale avec tous ses Vésuves éteints

It is not Switzerland, it's more awe-inspiring, it is not Italy, it's more beautiful, it is central France with all its extinct Vesuviuses.

George Sand

A high, tough and hauntingly beautiful land of eighty extinct volcanoes, Auvergne is the strong heart of France. Separated from the milder lowlands by its walls of rock and the poverty of its soil, it was long a battleground for fierce warlords, local and invading. The peasants and clergy were subjected to unbridled civil violence and the towns to a form of protection racket, the Church their only anchor. At the end of the tenth century, riding on a deep fear of holy relics and the first millennium shared by peasants and nobles alike, the bishops of Auvergne launched a religious and social process, called the Peace of God (Pax Dei), to bring an end to these devastating private wars. The process gradually spread from Auvergne into the rest of extenuated feudal Europe.

Religious fervour has left superb abbeys and churches, many named after Auvergne's founder saints (St Flour, Ste Foy (though her relics were actually brought by stealth from Agen in 866), St Nectaire). Outstanding examples of Romanesque architecture with some stunning carving and statuary, they alone are worth a week in Auvergne. Some prefer the lovely old watering places such as Vichy, Vals les Bains or Chaudes Aigues where modern spas pump the waters, hot, mineral or sulphurous, from the volcanoes.

The region remained poor, the people scraping a living from a cow or two on the moorland pastures, a pig in the yard and a few hardy vegetables. Fortunately, the woods provided (they still do) chestnuts, mushrooms and sweet summer fruits such as blueberries and raspberries. Traditional recipes tell it all, many dishes consisting of potatoes, garlic and cheese (aligot: potato purée with melted cheese and garlic; truffade: another way of doing potatoes, cheese and garlic with bacon) or are essentially made of vegetables (potée auvergnate: cabbage, carrots, potatoes and a bit of pork if one can afford it).

From the start of the industrial age, the Auvergne sent its sons to seek their fortunes in the cities. Typical immigrant workers, they started at the bottom of the ladder as cold-water carriers, then suppliers of hot baths (carrying bath, cold water and hot up... and down again once the client had bathed), then coal merchants and purveyors of cheap wine, while sending most of their earnings home. The Auvergne's most famous sons are the Michelin dynasty, heroes of the twentieth century adventure. In 1891, the Michelin brothers invented the removable bicycle tyre. Soon, they were selling car tyres, publishing guides (the world-famous Guide Rouge first came out in 1900), even making enamelled road signs. The Auvergne entices visitors with eye-popping panoramas from its eroded mountain tops, deep lush valleys where old castles hide, and underpopulated, unspoilt stretches of wilderness where walking, fishing and bird-watching are so rewarding.

[AUVERGNE]

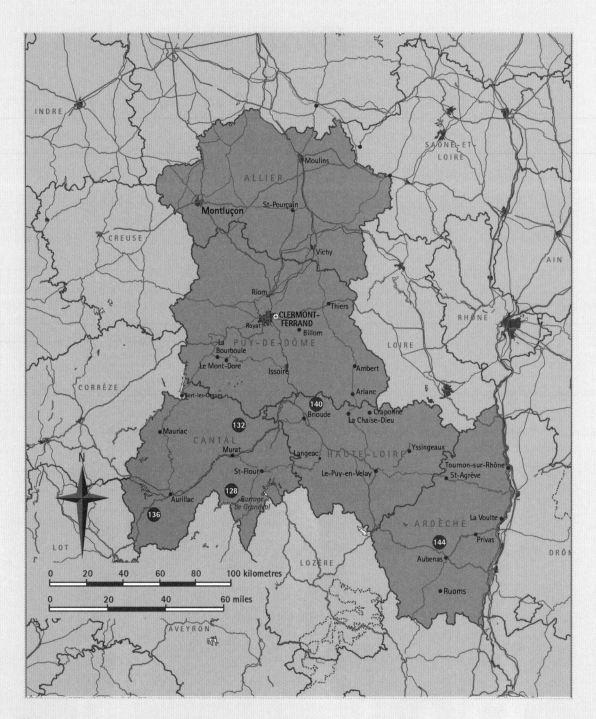

INDRE

SAÔNE-ET-LOIRE

Moulins

ALLIER

CREUSE

Montluçon

St-Pourçain

Vichy

RHÔNE

AIN

Riom

Thiers

CLERMONT-FERRAND

Royat

Billom

LOIRE

La PUY-DE-DÔME
Bourboule

Le Mont-Dore

Issoire

Ambert

CORRÈZE

Bort-les-Orgues

Arlanc

140

Brioude

Craponne

La Chaise-Dieu

132

Mauriac

CANTAL

Murat

Langeac

HAUTE-LOIRE

Yssingeaux

St-Flour

Le-Puy-en-Velay

Tournon-sur-Rhône

St-Agrève

128

Aurillac

Barrage
de Grandval

136

ARDÈCHE

La Voulte

Privas

144

DRÔ

LOT

Aubenas

N

LOZÈRE

Ruoms

| 0 | 20 | 40 | 60 | 80 | 100 kilometres |

| 0 | 20 | 40 | 60 miles |

AVEYRON

Special places to stay

Auvergne

Rhône Valley - Alps

Château de Lescure

AUVERGNE

Lescure is part of the very bones of Auvergne. One of the oldest houses in the province, its original defence tower dating from the eleventh century and its rock-solid 'auvergnate' farmhouse from the fifteenth, it is made of volcanic stone, timber and roof shingles extracted from the land it stands on, part of Europe's largest volcanic mass.

Since retiring to Sophie's family home from his life as a globe-trotting engineer, Michel has thrown himself into the minutiae of local history, marrying investigation on the ground and internet research. He works through the winter in the county archives or by the great inglenook fireplace, "though I have to admit that my computer occasionally fails me, its innards tarred up by smoke or the fan unable to cope with the heat."

They are both avid walkers and Michel uses his experience of international negotiation to persuade the local powers-that-be to provide support. Those powers now contribute to the mapping and marking of long-hidden pilgrim and trading paths and the development of soft tourism and access to nature. The aim is to bring visitors to wild unspoilt Auvergne in small groups, harmlessly walking these ancient pathways, kayaking on beautiful mountain rivers and enjoying the hot springs they call "gifts from the volcanoes" (at Chaudes Aigues, the water rises at 82°C, the hottest in Europe).

Our hosts had just returned from a four-day "experimental hike", exploring a 1,000-year-old path between the eagle's nest of Turlande Lescure and La Chaise Dieu, in the footsteps (they believe) of the abbey-builder Saint Robert de Turlande. Born in 1001, this child of the millennium, a monk and a great-hearted man, founded an abbey on a barren, snow-blasted rock like the place he was born. The foundation spawned offspring all over Europe. La Casa Dei (house of God, its name deformed to

Chaise from the medieval French) is now home to a superb gothic abbey and a world-famous sacred music festival.

The uncovering of Robert's route revealed "fabulous landscapes, ruined monastic buildings, stone sarcophagi deep in the forest, including those of children taught by the monks. Coming off these ancient trails into La Chaise Dieu, mind and body tuned to a different rhythm, we were shocked by the town, by the noise of civilisation." Guests sometimes go with them on such pioneering hikes.

In this tough unyielding land, life was hard and people had to rely on their own resources. At Lescure, summer heat and winter freeze were softened by the natural insulation of the spongy volcanic stone – and still are. "The stuff is like pumice, encrusted with stones gathered up by the lava as it rolled down from the crater."

It makes, too, for fertile soil. Michel and Sophie encourage their rare apple varieties through the rigours of this mountain valley and are proud members of the Cantal society of apple eaters (Association des Croqueurs de Pommes du Cantal). Sophie, passionate about food, will only accept the purest, most natural ingredients. She, Michel and the myriad Wwoofers* (farm volunteers) they have welcomed over the years have laid the kitchen garden out like a medieval monastic potager with a pond, a solar fountain, wicker borders and 'industrial' plants such as flax and hemp, as well as edible and medicinal varieties. The strong contemplative vein deepens each time the gardener lifts her eyes to the lovely valley that sweeps away from the edge of the garden; here she grows vegetables and their companion plants, the flowers that put a smile on her salads. Like so many of us, she has to wage the unending battle against bindweed, blaming climate change for its ever-increasing vigour.

"I love making soups with my garden produce and things foraged in the woods. In early summer, the dish of the day is Green Soup made with nettles, radish tops, spring leeks; salads may include wild plantains. In winter, we string our legs of lamb

up to roast slowly over the open fire, just as they did in the Middle Ages." She dreams of old-style self sufficiency. "Our local cheese-maker produces more butter cream than he knows what do so with

> "One of the oldest houses in the province, its original defence tower dating from the eleventh century and its rock-solid 'auvergnate' farmhouse from the fifteenth"

so I make my own butter, in old moulds from Brittany." She has poultry, too, including Marans hens "that lay the golden eggs" (actually a rich dark russet). Some hens fall victim to raiding foxes but Lescure has adopted the local philosophy of "la part du renard": allowing the fox to take his share.

A great knitter, Sophie was taught to spin and card her own wool by an English expert, but he said her spinning wheel was impossibly antique. So she bought a new one, a Polish model, from bohemian Brits in Dordogne... and while she spins and knits, Michel weaves medieval tales of barbarous barons and evangelising monks or, later, Queen Margot's nineteenth lover and the literary salon she held while imprisoned in her château by her king of a husband.

* Wwoofers - see notes on p. 242

Michel Couillaud & Phoebe Sophie Verhulst

Château de Lescure, 15230 St Martin Sous Vigouroux
- 3: 1 twin; 1 double with separate shower,
  1 double with separate shower room downstairs.
- €85-€90. Extra person €20.
- Dinner with wine, €20-€28. Children €10.
- +33 (0)4 71 73 40 91
- sites.google.com/site/chateaudelescure
- Train station: Saint Flour

Ferme des Prades

AUVERGNE

Cantal, the old volcanic heart of remote rocky Auvergne, remains detached from mainstream France despite the magnificent motorway that was built 'to open it up', and winter snowdrifts may leave villages stranded for days. Laid across the lava-spread hills, its rolling green pastures and thick dark woods seem to have more cattle than people; you can walk for miles in the beauty and never meet a soul.

Or take the Vélo-Rail. Prades is on the Cézallier plateau, a region of lush summer pastures where the cattle are brought when the grazing down below shrivels in the ovens of summer. In the mid-1800s, the railways arrived and the cattle were brought to their summer pastures by train instead of being driven up the thousand metres on foot. In the mid-1900s, roads and lorries arrived to do the job and the railways were abandoned; many hamlets, too, now stand in ruins as the population drain empties the Cantal of its residents. Not entirely, though. Tourism brings new people every year and some of the old 'transhumance' railway lines now carry pedal-carts that visitors can ride, freewheeling down and pedalling back up, the wind in their hair, the birdsong in their ears as they bundle through the glorious views.

Built of big volcanic stones with the small windows characteristic of Auvergnat architecture, hunkered down into the earth against the elements, the farmhouse is actually

a solid, compact château that opens out Tardis-like into huge rooms. Destroyed in the French Revolution, it was rebuilt by Napoleon's confessor, an archbishop whose portrait in scarlet hangs on the landing and who ordained that it should have glossy floorboards, solid timbers, generous fireplaces and window seats for contemplation. When it was Françoise's turn, she undertook to paint the kitchen cupboards with a delightful collection of lively poultry personalities and turn five rooms into seductive farmhouse bedrooms for guests.

The Vauchés, a warm, unpretentious and down-to-earth couple, grew up in the world of animal husbandry but no longer have their own herd, just taking two hundred 'boarders' for the summer. The rich milk from these high pastures and generations of quiet work have made the region famous for its Appellation Contrôlée cheeses: Cantal, Salers, Saint Nectaire, Bleu d'Auvergne. There are dairy farmers nearby who still make their own cheeses and Françoise takes guests on fascinating visits to these "committed artisans who are saving the reputation of French cheese in the face of tasteless mass-produced imitations."

She and Philippe love having people in the vast rambling house, as their sons are away studying and the farm is the sum total of the

hamlet of Prades, its nearest neighbours being kilometres away. "When I decided to buy my siblings' shares in the family house and had to make it pay, I knew it was made for B&B. The idea came naturally. And as I had watched my mother and grandmother

> "Make the slow-cooked traditional farmhouse dishes she learnt at her mother's elbow – stuffed cabbage, chicken with chestnut purée, Auvergne sausages baked with lentils..."

cooking here all my life, the idea of preparing meals and putting them on the table was obvious, too." She sources and cooks as they did. The naturally fertile pastures of the plateau call for little chemical treatment and at 1,100 metres altitude the air is pure, "as shown by the quantities of bees," says Françoise. "We have a market gardener down in the valley, a free-range poultry farmer in a nearby village ("the fox ate all my chickens last year so I've given up rearing my own"), a butcher selling superb Salers beef and a honey supplier in Allanche."

These are the fresh local ingredients she uses to make the slow-cooked traditional farmhouse dishes she learned at her mother's elbow – stuffed cabbage, chicken with chestnut purée, Auvergne sausages baked with lentils, 'truffade', a wonderful mixture of potatoes, fresh Cantal cheese and cream. Meanwhile, Philippe may be grilling hunks of meat over the dining-room fire or pouring his own chestnut cordial for the local version of kir, the festive table ready behind him.

As a little girl, Françoise used to stir the milk in the cheese-making room on the ground floor and her bedside tables made of old pottery milk churns brim with memories of that vanished past. She remembers the village 'rebouteux' (bonesetter) whose peasant hands could remove warts, cool burns and repair sprains, just with their gnarled touch. She now sits on

the town council but finds it hard to get new ideas accepted. "For twenty-four years, the farmers refused to have a footpath marked, saying that visitors would let the cattle out. They have to understand that if we don't welcome outsiders, we'll have no more shops and will just be providing services for the elderly. I'd also like the people here, especially the children, to understand why we must protect the environment."

She and Philippe care that town-dwellers get a real taste of the Auvergne and its extraordinary beauty. In the autumn, they organise hikes to hear the rutting stags or to gather mushrooms and come home for a cookery lesson; in winter, there's snow-shoe hiking, and in spring the astonishing wealth of wildflowers is irresistible.

An ancient local saying declares that "La France, c'est l'Auvergne avec quelque chose autour" (France is the Auvergne with something around it.) Just look at a map.

Françoise & Philippe Vauché

Ferme des Prades,
Les Prades, Landeyrat, 15160 Allanche
- 5: 3 doubles, 2 family rooms.
- €67-€72.
- Dinner with wine, €20.
- +33 (0)4 71 20 48 17
- www.fermedesprades.com
- Train station: Allanche

Auberge de Concasty

AUVERGNE

As far as the eye can reach, one swelling line of hilltops rises and falls behind another.
Travels with a donkey in the Cévennes
Robert Louis Stevenson

Half a mile above sea level, the great Cantal landscape rolls away from Concasty's plateau perch to woods, pastures and distant hills. For many years, this former notary's mansion was the Causse family's farmhouse. Then, in their fifties, Martine's parents went for a holiday in Alsace, discovered *le tourisme rural* and decided to open their own house so that others could share their stupendous views, pure air and healthy Cantal food. Martine took over twenty years ago and has modernised the place without gainsaying the original philosophy of personal contact and care for all living things. The latest example, the former chestnut dryer or Sécadou, has been transformed into a gorgeous suite.

"Slow time is a part of life in the Auvergne," says Martine. "Much of this house was built a hundred and fifty years ago. The boundary wall was the work of day labourers who used to travel the region looking for jobs. They would stop at building sites, collect stones for the masonry and do some rough building in exchange for board and lodging. That wall was done little by little and without cement."

Farming is of the older, slower type, too. Cattle roam the hillsides,

the hardier being left out through the long winters. Martine buys local, free-range meat "but seldom our famous Salers. That almost all goes up to the city markets and there's nothing left for us, the 'Auvergnats d'Auvergne'. Our farmers grow their own wheat and maize for cattle feed using very little fertiliser (though they're not labelled organic). This means that our water is not contaminated with nitrates. It's ironic that what used to be the obvious, normal way of doing things now carries a certificate that costs €3,000 a year! The local dairy farm has Jersey cows, their wonderful rich milk has always been sold in glass bottles and pots and the farm is converting to organic, but the cost of certification is heavy for them."

With the cleanest air, water and soil in the country, the Auvergne is eager to shout about its low pollution levels. Martine has more to say about modern food production methods: "We read that milk is hard for humans to digest but the culprit is pasteurisation, it kills the protein that makes milk easily digestible. The Auvergnat's approach to farming is respectful of nature and we treat our animals well. My nephew, who farms next door, is gentle with his cattle – he walks his one-ton bull the way I walk my dog – and he grows, organically, the vegetables that we don't have in our potager so our

meals are essentially chemical-free." Omar, who grew up in Morocco and is Martine's partner in the business, seconds her opinion on cow's milk. "I remember coming home from school, throwing my satchel down and running round to my grandmother's for a bowl of milk straight from the cow." As Concasty's sommelier, he is much appreciated by wine buffs.

Guests are asked to send towels to wash only when needed, the water is naturally soft so less washing powder is used than normal, the linen is folded straight from the dryer, bypassing the ironing stage and saving energy. "Even with twelve rooms, we are more 'chambres et table d'hôtes' than hotel.

> "With the cleanest air, water and soil in the country, the Auvergne is eager to shout about its low pollution levels"

People come here for peace and quiet and we spend time with them finding the right things to do for each person, making sure they don't miss the smaller treasures. There are superb walks from our door."

With their mountain climate and manual labour on the farms, rural folk expect solid fuel before the day's work. Concasty's Auvergnat breakfast will keep you going for hours with its charcuterie, vegetable salad, fruit salad, breads, pastries and homemade jams. The evening brings a single menu of fresh vegetables and tasty local specialities, the epitome of 'table d'hôtes', prepared by Martine and her brother Robert in the neat, calm kitchen. A child may come in from building a den and ask for a glass of milk while the home-grown raspberry mousse is being whipped into shape.

As well as meeting, greeting and serving in the restaurant, Omar gives massage and stretching sessions. "Massage is a traditional Moroccan way of treating pain and stress. I have also learned Ayurvedic and other eastern methods that use breathing to support the hands in their job of unloading the body's negative pressures and balancing its energy. I love being here, the gentleness of things, the contact with people. We take time to listen to them, to win their trust, and often get into interesting philosophical conversations. And I love the Auvergne; it has some of the untouched wilderness feel of Morocco."

"We have lots of repeat guests," says Martine, "it's marvellous, they feel like family. Some regularly walk their dogs in their bathrobes, others play chess on the terrace for hours, or swim three times a day in the glass-screened pool (a clever and stylish response to the EC safety directive). I just wish that, instead of crowding onto the beaches, more people would stop and make time for the experience of real life that we offer, far from the agitated cities."

Martine Causse

Auberge de Concasty, 15600 Boisset
- 12: 11 doubles, 1 family room.
- €63–€127.
- Breakfast €9. Brunch €16. Picnic available. Dinner €32–€42. Half-board €40 p.p
- +33 (0)4 71 62 21 16
- www.auberge-concasty.com
- Train station: Aurillac

Auberge de Chassignolles

AUVERGNE

The old village lay untouched, its 1930s inn decaying gently behind the medieval church, the ruins of the thirteenth-century castle crumbling next door, the population ageing as the young left the hills and pastures for city excitements.

Harry and Ali were young Londoners, he in the vanguard of the gastropub and artisan food movement, she a silversmith and design teacher. They enjoyed the buzz of creativity, fashion and success. Then Fred was born and their life plan changed. A chance encounter in a café told them of an old inn for sale in remotest Auvergne, and they moved to Chassignolles (pop. 18). "We've always been a bit rash, you see, and we'd gathered a few pennies, so off we set in search of direct contact with nature and closer relationships with food producers and their wares." Harry gives 'food honesty' his top priority. He was a Slow Food member for a time but now says he is "slow by definition not membership: slow means integrity and no short cuts, celebrating the real, leaving aside the PR of labels created by producers to protect producers."

Three years in and initially wary locals, who'd been instantly happy when the village bar reopened but were uneasy about eating anything that wasn't French, especially if cooked by an Englishman, have been won round by Harry's cooking. "I love the age-old French respect for food ingredients and preparation. Another beautiful thing about France is that all classes eat and enjoy the same things." On the other hand, he occasionally finds that European regulations weigh heavy on daily life. "I believe in doing what you want how you want," says Harry, "and England was possibly easier for that."

Ali finds her life here "quite normal now, quite self-contained with two small children, a radius of sixty kilometres, a business to build according to our ideals. We've only been back to England twice in three years. Our pace of life has changed so much that London's vibes seem alien; it's unimaginable, now, to live like that. We feel very privileged and we love sharing it."

They chose to keep the rooms as simple and natural as possible, each slightly different with polished floorboards, white bed linen, interesting old furniture and good plain bathrooms. Sheets are washed in house then aired and bleached in the sun; soaps are hand-made locally. There's a reading room for the young and less-than-young on the first floor.

The meadow-cum-orchard where guests are offered deckchairs from which to admire the view is where the sheep and hens – your dinner – live. You can take picnics and rugs on walks or ride bikes into the country and spend a day just being in the area. "Everyone slows down in response to our own pace, seeing us hang the washing out, Fred bringing a bunch of flowers for the restaurant, eating the kind of food Harry cooks, the neighbours walking over to open the church."

Ali is clear about recycling and sustainability. "We celebrate living frugally yet well, without excesses or luxuries. We are anti-throwaway and if we don't take a cardboard box to put the chickens in, our poultry lady is in despair about finding another. A plastic box is to be guarded with your life!"

The auberge is a mushroom exchange – another central service that Ali and Harry have revived – and harvesters bring in fantastic mountains of beautiful cèpes and chanterelles, each from their secret patch in the woods. "We check them, weigh them, pay the day's rate and the wholesaler packs them off to markets in Paris and London."

Direct food sourcing is natural here. All the inn's vegetables are grown organically for them in the valley. "I just go down to Yvan, see what's ready

"Everyone slows down in response to our own pace, seeing us hang the washing out, Fred bringing a bunch of flowers for the restaurant, eating the kind of food Harry cooks"

today – he grows rare varieties as well as typically regional things – and bring my choice up to the kitchen. He doesn't pay for certification yet I know it's organic and it's half the price of bio-labelled sources. People who don't spend their lives working with food need the guidance of labels but should beware of the Appellation Contrôlée tag; its cloud of mystique often covers industrial rubbish totally devoid of spirit. I buy only artisan cheeses and now have my own cheese room. The Neal's Yard Dairy man, who created Stichelton and has transformed the face of British cheese, says it's perfect..."

"Buying locally shouldn't be a fad," he says, "it should be a way of life. It creates links, strengthens

a community and builds friendships. We have become friends with our neighbours, too, and learned so much from them about looking after our livestock and land."

For breaking down barriers and building up business, Fred, now five, has been the best possible ambassador. They now do school feasts ("the approachable exotic type: paella one year, couscous the next"), the village's annual lunch, meals for groups (farmers, hunters, veterans, seniors), and people who used to walk past without ever coming in are now having birthdays, even wedding parties, here. Tripe is a favourite. The mayor came with twenty-five others for a breakfast meeting about the water supply and chose tripe, cherry tart and rosé.

Harry's main dishes are often for sharing among several people, "recalling convivial family mealtimes." When we dined, the appetiser was an anchoïade dip with raw carrots and radishes en branche just dug from the potager, leaves and tails still attached – out of this world. Guests can even bring in the fruits of their foraging for Harry to cook.

An antidote to urban frenzy, with a small grocery shop by the bar and thoughtful, deeply committed owners, this simple auberge is a perfect focus for revived community life and a boon for travellers.

Harry Lester & Ali Johnson

Auberge de Chassignolles, Le Bourg, 43440 Chassignolles
- 8: 6 doubles, 1 family room for 4, 1 twin.
- €45-€65.
- Breakfast €7.50. Lunch €24 (Sunday only).
  Dinner €24 (except Monday). Picnic €8.
- +33 (0)4 71 76 32 36
- www.aubergedechassignolles.com
- Train station: Brioude

Château Clément

RHÔNE VALLEY - ALPS

'It is the kind of place that has no flat land at all. Village after village is located underneath some steep valley floor next to a fast-flowing stream, surrounded by profuse vegetation. Roads curve crazily as they make their way up and down the hills, running past narrow, semicircular terraces buttressed by millions of stone ramparts.' Thus wrote Richard Bernstein twenty years ago. Had he visited the Ardèche a full hundred years ago instead of just twenty, he would have seen and felt the same countryside; and it is still the same today.

Before 1860, among the remote folds of these 'green craggy hills' in the heart of Ardèche, Vals les Bains was a place where people – not many, not fashionable (except Madame de Sévigné's daughter in the seventeenth century) – came to take the waters; chestnut woods covered the hills surrounding the sleepy town. Then Auguste Clément, 'a foreigner' from just across the Rhône, arrived to develop the spa, improve the hotels, beautify the town and spread the word to the world of takers of water. With the help of the wondrous railways, Vals became internationally famous for its therapeutic waters and Clément made enough money to buy and clear one of the hilltops and build himself this fairytale château.

After its glory years, it fell on hard times, falling so low as to be used as a 'secure residence' for political opponents during the Second World War, then a holiday camp for forty years, then left empty again, visited only by looters.

When Marie-Antoinette's parents fell under its spell in the 1990s, the château had been stripped of fireplaces, floorboards and statues, the hilly parkland was "a tangled jungle beneath the magnificent old trees, all the fountains whisked away." But it was still a real château with its unashamedly baronial double staircase and high moulded ceilings. Recovery, however, was a monumental task. Éric and Marie-Antoinette have achieved wonders – and a laudably eco-friendly place to stay. All the insulation and decorating were done with natural materials. As there is nowhere to site a wood-chip store, they are planning to install solar panels, and almost all their food comes from their own kitchen garden and local or organic suppliers.

Since they met working at a famous hotel in England, he a pastry cook, she a hotel management student, they had wanted to bring their children up in a natural, healthy environment. They found it at Château Clément. Children who come as guests adopt the place instantly, delighting in the relaxed family atmosphere, the great spaces for games and adventures, the suppers with Pauline (nine), Louise (six) and Constance (three) at their own table. Constance and baby Clovis were born in the château and

their mother eagerly describes the wonders of a natural home birth "to horrified women who think it's a mad, bad and dangerous idea."

Pauline's classmates come, too, for an annual look-taste-and-learn tour of the potager and chicken run, for a chocolate-tasting afternoon with Éric during the Semaine du Goût*, and the chance to realise that the Chabots are not the idle rich, that they really work here and are building for the future. Renovation continues on the outbuildings, the latest additions being a fitness room and hammam at The Loft. The Loft is the stylish contemporary house in the woods above the château where families or groups can stay to work or play in their own space and château guests can book sessions.

From the potager, which is the careful work of Marie-Antoinette's parents, Éric takes his vegetables, saved from pests by the famously stinking 'purin d'ortie' (macerated nettles). "I trained as a pastry cook but I enjoy doing starters now, mixing textures and highlighting the taste of each ingredient. I do a single menu each evening so that I can be completely organised and dine with our guests." He does Ardèche specialities such as Croustillant de Picodon (goat's cheese in pastry), and potato-based peasant dishes inspired by the tough living conditions of the past, but coming from Normandy he needs fish to be part of the plan, too. Fortunately, a fishmonger cousin in nearby Aubenas provides the best Breton mussels, for example, to go with the château's mini-courgettes. "My poultry lives and breeds in a neighbour's kiwi orchard and I revel in the very local, rare Violine de Borée potato with its chestnutty flavour. It used to be considered fit only for pigs but it's delicious, sweet enough to be used as a pudding ingredient yet a perfect foil for certain savoury dishes."

People who want to dine out are pointed towards two or three good restaurants, lent a torch and shown the path down to the town – it's just five hundred metres.

When they have a moment to spare, Éric and Marie sneak off to the grotto that Auguste Clément

built in the park, a restful spot where a spring rises, goldfish amble and people read, picnic or play gentle games on the lawn. Guest families come back regularly; they say the place is "magical yet real, run by a young family with children whose joie-de-vivre is catching." Marie-Antoinette's comment is: "I love the way lives slide into one another like this so that we can watch each other's children grow as they come back year after year." They know, too, that people are looking for more contact and conviviality than anonymous hotels can offer. "We feel humbled by the people we meet and the encounters among guests that Château Clément makes possible. We consider this a collective project: our family, the guests and this wonderful place all working together."

* Semaine du Goût - see notes on p. 242

Marie-Antoinette & Éric Chabot

Château Clément,
La Châtaigneraie, 07600 Vals les Bains
- 5 + 2: 4 doubles, 1 suite. Apt for 4. Loft for 8-10.
- €160-€250. Apt €1,500-€2,000. Loft €2,500-€3,800 p.w.
- Dinner with wine, €60.
- +33 (0)4 75 87 40 13
- www.chateauclement.com
- Train station: Montelimar

[LANGUEDOC - ROUSSILLON]

Jadis apprivoisé par les Romains et se mirant dans les eaux turquoises où naissent les huitres, les robustes vignobles puisent toute la sève de ce pays brillant des chaudes couleurs méditerranéennes

Tamed by the Romans long ago, mirrored in the turquoise waters where oysters grow, the hardy vines draw up the full sap of this land, shining with hot Mediterranean colours.

Label of Picpoul de Pinet 1997

Spread between the peaks of the Catalan Pyrenees, the Cévennes and the Mediterranean, Languedoc-Roussillon is a strong, demanding land of rugged hills, dazzling light in hot dry summers and violent winds (Mistral and Tramontane) in winter. The vegetation has evolved to survive: low-lying, water-frugal garrigue (scrubland) on the coastal plains and hills, evergreen oak and mountain ash in the woodlands. Vines have always prospered in the poor soil and hot sun of the lowlands; further inland, mountain torrents push their way through stupendous gorges. The Romans occupied the region in -120 BC and stayed for six centuries, growing wine, taking baths, building roads and leaving some monumental souvenirs when they 'retired': amphitheatres and arches and, above all, the astounding 2,000-year-old Pont du Gard. This mighty aqueduct's only real rival in the region is the magical twentieth-century road bridge that floats over the Tarn at Millau.

The region is sometimes called the poor man's Provence, a reputation that has kept it blessedly free of celebrity cultists and mafia wealth. Life is slow, the old people sit out to watch the world go by and play innumerable games of pétanque while the street markets ring with the cries of cheese-makers from Aveyron, trout fishers from the Cévennes and potters from St Jean de Fos, renowned for ceramics since the 1300s.

Marie Gaches, a local poetess, has compared the villages of the Haut Languedoc to scattered sheep: "How can one bring the flock together? There is no one spot where the whole village can be seen. One or two groups of houses are always missing; it's like the zen gardens of Kyoto: wherever you stand, your eye can never pick up all the stones." A village will line the banks of the stream or huddle round the fountain in the shade of the gentle plane trees. Each house will have a great arch opening onto a *remise* where the wine was, sometimes still is, made and stored; living happens upstairs. The wine trade is in distress now, overtaken by competition from the New World, but orchards still flourish and olive groves are planted where vines are dug up. Alternatively, younger wine-growers are turning to organic and bio-dyamic methods, aiming to survive in the modern market.

This is, unforgettably, a land of food, too. Mussels grown on the coast are barbecued *en brasucade du Languedoc* with aromatic oil; the highland streams carry lively wild trout, their lower reaches are home to perch and pike; and sheep graze freely on the herb-laden hillsides providing milk for Roquefort and meat for gourmets.

Culture of all sorts flourishes at hundreds of festivals and in the theatres and museums, operas and concert halls of Montpellier, Perpignan, Nîmes, Pézenas and many more old towns with a modern outlook.

[LANGUEDOC – ROUSSILLON]

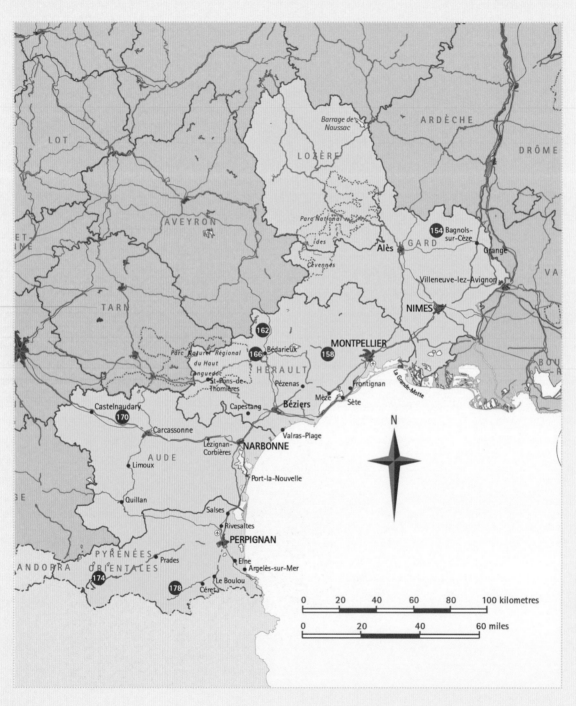

LOT

AVEYRON

TARN

ARDÈCHE

DRÔME

LOZÈRE

Barrage de Naussac

Parc National
ides
Cèvennes

Alès

GARD

154 Bagnols-sur-Cèze

Orange

Villeneuve-lez-Avignon

VA

NÎMES

162

166 Bédarieux

Parc Naturel Régional du Haut Languedoc

St-Pons-de-Thomières

MONTPELLIER

158

HÉRAULT

Pézenas

Mèze

Frontignan

La Grande-Motte

BOU

Sète

Castelnaudary

170

Carcassonne

Capestang

Béziers

AUDE

Limoux

Lézignan-Corbières

NARBONNE

Valras-Plage

Port-la-Nouvelle

Quillan

Salses

Rivesaltes

PERPIGNAN

N

PYRÉNÉES ORIENTALES

ANDORRA

Prades

Elne

Argelès-sur-Mer

174

178

Céret

Le Boulou

| 0 | 20 | 40 | 60 | 80 | 100 kilometres |

| 0 | 20 | 40 | 60 miles |

Special places to stay

Languedoc – Roussillon

La Magnanerie

GARD

This is glorious walking country. Some call it the Cévennes foothills, some call it the Gard Provençal. It is beautiful by any name with its wild landscape of rugged hills studded with green oak woods, steep limestone valleys carved over five million years by erosion and glaciers into cliffs and giants' cauldrons, gorges and rapids. When the River Aiguillon dries up in summer, the Concluses de Lussan (narrows or gorges) are a spectacular sight from the bottom of the gorge, well worth the tough scramble down – but don't scramble alone.

Surrounded by vineyards, lavender fields and aromatic garrigue, Fons is a typical stone village that was several hundred years old when the Genvrins' *magnanerie* (silk farm) was built in the eighteenth century. For such a tiny settlement – one hundred and seventy-five residents in winter – it is remarkable in having a well-stocked shop run by a dynamic young woman who took the business over from her mother,

restored it to its old-style rustic prettiness, buys from local market gardeners and sells organic produce. Her Épicerie Fonsoise is one of the pillars of village life. The other is the lively, convivial bar where everyone meets for coffee or a drink. "We all greet each other and look out for one another," says Michèle. "People are so much more relaxed here than in the north where I used to live."

After eleven years in Fons, Michèle and Michel belong to the village. He sits on the council and she runs art classes, including one for the village children and one for autistic teenagers from the local centre. "It's amazing what these youngsters can achieve through art and I find it terrifically rewarding to hand on the gifts I have received." As a decorative artist, Michèle is faithful to the past, painting on wood and fabric and using old-fashioned and rediscovered ingredients such as natural sap resin and glue made from animal skins. Her bedside reading is the 'Libro

dell'Arte' by quattrocento Florentine artist Cennino Cennini. Appreciative students feel thoroughly at home in her peaceful studio as they learn how to decorate their houses and furniture. One of them is Annat, the local woman blacksmith who makes a fast-selling Slow snail.

Cooking is another of Michèle's passions and, as with her painting, she needs to take time over it. Without a potager of her own, she contributes to the village herb and tomato garden. "I would rather eat our little tomatoes grown naturally in the sun than overblown synthetic rubbish from Spain. The taste of the real thing reminds me of my father's tomatoes. It's the sweet taste of summer and if you get them straight from the source they don't cost any more. We have lots of little pick-your-own places here for fruit and vegetables." There's local organic goat's cheese, too. "The farm is just outside the village so a satisfying walk is involved, as well as good food at the end. Their delicious cheeses are totally different from industrial dairy products."

Guests sleep in colourful bedrooms and join quite naturally in the family's life. "We're not acting any roles, we are as we are and our house is just our house, without pretensions, not perfect, not designer finished, but people seem to like being here."

Michel restores old buildings using, as far as the owners will allow, eco-friendly materials and methods: lime wash and old-style paints, second-hand doors and fireplaces that he gets from reclamation yards. "The authentic takes time," he says, "and I am always delighted when clients understand that this is the right way. People are too often in a hurry or short of money and I know concrete is cheaper and quicker than stone." His seat on the council allows him to steer the authorities towards better planning and regulating of old and new building. "He's a charming and persuasive communicator," says Michèle.

Their typical silk farm had the farm animals on the ground floor, the family's living quarters on the first floor with one enclosed and one open terrace and on the second floor, in what is now the sitting room, the silk-producing workshop. In one part they stored the hay and the mulberry leaves, in another room was

the silkworm nursery with a little fireplace in each corner. The weather can be chilly here in March, which is when the worms hatch, so fires were laid to keep the eggs warm. Michèle tells of their experiment when they first arrived. "We grew a few worms in a shoe box. They don't move at all and when they've finished their leaves they let themselves die. We fed them until they became as fat as fingers and started to lift their heads but we didn't manage to provide the right shelter for them to spin their cocoons."

Silk production lasted here until the 1950s. A cocoon contains three kilometres of silk. Three of these threads would be spun into one at the local

> "It is beautiful by any name
> with its wild landscape of
> rugged hills studded
> with green oak woods"

factory then the spools sent to Lyon for the luxury textile business. "At least when the silk growers left to work in the more lucrative mines, their villages were not replaced by concrete estates. Our house became the local Catholic café. The other one was Protestant – and scarcely the twain did meet!"

Such was life in the Cévennes not very long ago. Stay today with this artistic and welcoming couple and you will taste old-style hospitality in an easier community spirit.

Michèle Dassonneville & Michel Genvrin

La Magnanerie,
Place de l'Horloge, 30580 Fons sur Lussan
- 4: 2 doubles, 2 family suites for 4.
- €55–€60.
- Dinner with wine, €20.
- +33 (0)4 66 72 81 72
- www.atelier-de-fons.com
- Train station: Nîmes

Domaine de Pélican

HÉRAULT

Thirty years ago, Isabelle left Mâcon to study tourism in Montpellier, dreaming of taking people to fabulous places all over the world. A holiday job took her thirty kilometres away to the Domaine de Pélican, the grape harvest, and Baudonin: she never left. Her one exotic journey has been to Morocco. "However, the rest of the world now comes to my door."

"I love this place," she says, "it's magical. It has been the perfect place to bring up our five children, I enjoy sharing it and I want to keep it beautiful. That view, sweeping away from the house, is my favourite, with the light and colours changing as sun and cloud lean over it. No wonder painters come, set up their gear and then can scarcely stop for dinner. I am on something of a mission to preserve the many riches of this untouched environment, creating a safe haven for wildlife and welcoming guests as if they were family." Brigades of birds, rabbits, squirrels and wild boar have settled in the no-shoot zone that she and Baudouin have set up.

The domaine has been in Baudouin's family for several generations. Three kilometres from the village, it was their *campagne* (a country estate with an unsophisticated house and a manager) and it was unthinkable to live here permanently when the only transport was the horse and carriage. The farm manager had a house, the shepherd had a sheepfold, the farm workers had a lodging house, and the owner rode out to check up from time to time. When Baudouin's father decided to come and live here, his son dropped his agricultural studies, joined him at Pélican and, learning it all from scratch, turned himself into a wine-grower. The buildings were in poor condition and the vineyard was an old-style get-as-much-as-you-can Languedoc operation.

Little by little, vines were pulled up and the vineyard restructured to give less quantity and more quality, "which means proper respect for the *terroir*," says Baudouin. "I follow *agriculture raisonnée* principles,

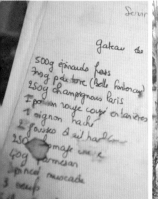

using a minimum of chemicals, leaving grasses to grow between the vines but avoiding the constraints and costs of a fully organic system. We aim for low yields and the clean soil I now work with gives the grapes a recognisable character. That individuality, of course, is what the *terroir* craze is all about." Isabelle adds: "In everything we do, we aim for balance rather than inaccessible perfection. After all, any extreme has its flip side. Ours is not a house for those seeking a designer finish!"

The estate has a twenty-five-hectare vineyard, the family house, the B&B outbuildings and a small summer camping site of a dozen pitches. Baudouin and Isabelle run it all themselves, the wine-making, the inn and the potager, with much willing help from their children in the high season. It has been hard work, managing and growing while rebuilding, but the family all pull together. As Isabelle describes it: "This is a lived-in house and we are immersed in the spontaneity of daily life, juggling children, guests, meals, the house, the vineyard... We can't foresee every detail in black and white and it can happen that rooms are not ready if guests arrive a bit early, but we're still delighted to see them." Early birds can always set off into the wild, scented garrigue, guided by Argane, the friendly collie. If you bring a baby with you, Argane will keep guard outside your room all night. The two cats are more distant, as befits their Siamese dignity.

"We keep things as simple and natural as possible. Slow and local have been my guides since we started our auberge and I believe in being realistic and honest. We used to have hens but either the foxes would get into the hen house or the dogs would bother them. I decided it was a waste of energy and have found the right poultry supplier; his guinea-fowl are never dry or stringy." They gather many of their fresh fruits in a big abandoned orchard nearby that still produces good harvests of peaches, pears, quinces, Morello cherries and figs.

Isabelle is an unusually happy cook. "My favourite recipes are for poultry and I often cook them with fresh fruit – guinea-fowl with Morello cherries is a fine, subtle mix of tastes. The auberge restaurant can be busy and buzzy but we enjoy it,

too, when guests get to know each other and want to go on talking round the table and the place takes on a house-party atmosphere."

This is an ancient, wild land. The twisty village of Saint Guilhem le Désert, built among the dry hills above the Hérault River gorge, was established as a hermitage in the eighth century by one of Charlemagne's companions, Guillaume de Toulouse. He renounced soldiering and worldly pursuits and founded an abbey whose history leaps over centuries and continents. To the despair of local fine-art lovers, sections of its beautiful twelfth-century cloister are still "held captive" by the Cloisters Museum in New York. For more active pleasures, the Hérault gorges and their (mild) rapids can be explored in kayaks, the Salagou lake offers swimming and sailing, oysters are to be eaten in fishing villages by the Étang de Thau, geological wonders to be seen in underground caves or reaching for the sky in Mourèze.

* Terroir - see notes on p. 242

Isabelle & Baudouin Thillaye du Boullay

Domaine de Pélican,
34150 Gignac
- 4: 2 doubles, 1 twin, 1 suite for 4.
- €62-€72.
- Dinner €24. Restaurant in village.
- +33 (0)4 67 57 68 92
- www.domainedepelican.fr
- Train station: Montpellier

La Voix du Ruisseau

HÉRAULT

Climb one of the 1,000-metre summits that surround Graissessac and you'll see the whole of the Haut Languedoc Park spread below you, the snow-capped Pyrenees beyond. This village tells the story of the region. It may look like any other inland Mediterranean settlement, its tiled houses spread along the banks of a little river running between mountain and forest, the rocks everlasting, the air clean, the water pure... but, like many places in the Languedoc, it has a hidden past. Coal was discovered here in the nineteenth century, transforming a lost mountain village into a lively mining community. You can still see signs of this eventful past in pit entrances, streets lined with townhouses and a great cliff that attracts geology students and people interested in the story of coal. Nature has since re-established its reign and the village has returned to its earlier, more peaceful state. You will pass rich vegetable gardens as you walk slowly through, meet friendly locals with time to chat, hear sheep bells calling from the hillsides.

Monika didn't come to Graissessac that day to learn about coal but to consult an osteopath – "and a woman in the high street informed me, out of the blue, that there was 'only one property left for sale in the village' (how did she know I might be looking for a

house, somewhere, some day?). Jim and I came back, took the hidden track out of the village, crossed the bridge, and discovered the very place we had been longing for. We felt guided."

'Quiet American' Jim, a fine guitarist and a songwriter "at the shimmering edge of the void" (his words) with a poet's inwardness, and Monika, a writer of *Prosastücke, kurz und länger* (prose pieces, short and long), who came from Germany many moons ago, dreamed of living sustainably, in harmony with nature, sharing their passions with others in a protected, contemplative environment. "Here was the very hillside, our sacred haven in the wilderness, stretching away from the house to wooded slopes of oak and chestnut fed by two streams, an ideal spot for yurts, but not cut off from the local community."

It took five years to build their dream, starting with a study of sustainable architecture. Jim and Monika cared deeply that any new building did nothing to disturb the natural beauty of the setting. The Japanese approach to building in landscape was one inspiration, *Building with the Breath of Life* was another. Yurts were the obvious answer and they pursued their plans to turn the house into an eco-friendly home and guest house, rehabilitate the potager and orchard as well as the existing rainwater harvesting and irrigation systems. They worked slowly and carefully, finding a radiesthesist (energy diviner) to help them define the best sites for the yurts and using only natural materials. The job was done by a highly skilled crew of builders and they remember with pleasure the young people who came to make thousands of earth bricks with a manual press. "All this needed time and we learned much from each other throughout the process."

The yurts were made with local, sustainably managed chestnut wood, bamboo from Anduze, canvas, hemp and seagrass. "Each stands in its own setting. The bigger, higher-domed yurt feels almost like a sacred space, the smaller one is like a sheltered nest suspended over the stream, while the communal kitchen, open to the majestic trees, is an invitation to communication and exchange." They also searched for eco-friendly solutions for the heating, hot water and drainage systems.

> "They dreamed of living sustainably, in harmony with nature, sharing their skills and passions with others in a protected, contemplative environment"

Monika enjoys cooking, spontaneously, "just taking what's in the garden as inspiration. A salad of rocket with finely sliced pears and shaved parmesan, followed by aubergines, mozzarella and tomatoes gratiné as a summer meal, or a simple potato salad with dandelion greens in spring. We are learning from our neighbours about all the edible wild herbs, fruits and mushrooms that grow here, some of them on our property." For several years, Monika and Jim sold home-cooked organic vegetarian dishes at local markets; now she uses this talent for occasional dinners with guests and enjoys having more writing time as their building

works come to an end. "This is a perfect place to write," she says, "to talk to the cat and grow untainted vegetables."

Early in the morning, she can be found in the potager. "I listen to the plants, trying to hear their will. Jim comes down on summer evenings to water each one in his contemplative fashion." Mitsu the tomcat, found as a kitten in the woods, is an essential member of the family. "He gives us affection and teaches us, wonderfully, about being in the moment."

"Being in the calm of this powerful place increases one's awareness." It is as perfect for Jim and Monika's quiet way of living as it is for guests staying in the yurts. There, they can sit peacefully or paint on their own terraces or walk out into the greenery. "As you rest in the comfortable simplicity of the fabric shelter," says Monika, "nature's sounds are immediately with you: the creek, whose voice full of meaning inspired the name we gave our property, twinkling down the hill to meet the stream, the nightingales in May, the barking of the deer or the wind falling down the valley, trying to shake the yurt like a wild animal."

The special summer coolness of this corner, the trees, grass and water, make it a haven when heat blisters city streets.

Jim Benton & Monika Sonntag

La Voix du Ruisseau, 16 rue de Riols, 34260 Graissessac
- 1 yurt for 5-6, 1 yurt for 2-3. Tent for children. Shower house & compost wc shared by all.
- €280-€350 per week. €70 B&B for 2.
- Breakfast €5-€10. Dinner €25, wine extra.
- +33 (0)9 51 36 50 54
- www.voixduruisseau.org
- Train station: Bédarieux

Le Couvent d'Hérépian

HÉRAULT

His mother used to blame the wind if the cake was undercooked: her electric oven was powered by the windmill outside the old farmhouse. Respect for old things comes naturally to Miguel Espada, child of a Languedoc family of architectural restorers. After excursions into finance, he married Cécile, the daughter of a wine-making family near Béziers. Their 'union of stone and terroir' and their shared attachment to this region drive the Garrigae Group that Miguel founded. Its purpose is to rescue the architectural heritage of the Languedoc-Roussillon by turning run-down properties into sustainable tourist places; the criteria are beauty, authenticity and deep roots in the local landscape and history. The financial secret is a leaseback investment scheme. They have extended a remote hamlet in an old vineyard, converted a wine warehouse by the Mediterranean and this convent (their first project), and are resuscitating an old distillery in Pézenas and a destitute village château.

The former convent is an organic part of the narrow streets of the old village of Hérépian, its high north wall standing eyeball to eyeball with the worn church tower; on the sunny side, the garden faces the wild hills that rise out of the Orb valley. Push the heavy door open onto sober grandeur. The barrel-vaulted, taupe-painted staircase that faces you is pure seventeenth-century convent, the glittering chandeliers are not: your first sense of the convent's melding of sobriety and hedonism.

Manager Fabrice Delprat lives just next door with his son and his cat Mistinguett. A quietly determined eco-warrier, he keeps the place on sustainable rails with humour and attention to detail. "I share Miguel Espada's instinct to convert rather than throw away. When we created the new pool (it looks like an eighteenth-century fishpond), I re-set the old fountain stones as semi-circular seats in the garden rather than sending them to the dump.

Instead of replacing the old pergolas with new ones, I had them straightened, repainted and replanted." He does his best to guide guests gently towards greener attitudes. "They send their towels to the wash less often than before but it's incredibly hard to get them to turn their lights off when they leave their rooms." Although water is heated by solar panels, the only system of central heating the designers could install in the old building was electrical. "But our radiant radiators are super-efficient and French electricity is increasingly provided by renewable and emission-free sources. You can see lots of wind farms in the Languedoc. Fortunately, double glazing and eighty-centimetre-thick old walls make air conditioning superfluous."

Fabrice plans to shrink the convent's eco-footprint yet further, reducing packaging and waste, for example, by handing out bathroom soaps and gels in returnable bottles.

The convent's big, square, high rooms in those muted nun's-habit tones are eco-quality showcases: pure Vosges linens, bamboo-fibre duvets, natural paints; bathrooms have the latest chic fittings on pebble floors, marble tiles and stone tops. The best rooms overlook the garden – a few have private terraces – and glow in the evening sun – while their north-facing sisters stay cool at all times.

Half way between Italy and Spain, the Languedoc has been an area of vineyards and constant to and fro since the Romans colonised Gaul. Later, pilgrims would find rest and shelter in the

> "Its purpose is to rescue the architectural heritage of the Languedoc-Roussillon by turning run-down properties into sustainable tourist venues; the criteria are beauty, authenticity and deep roots in the local landscape and history"

many abbeys that sprang up along the road to Compostela; the convent at Hérépian was a small part of this story. It was built in the seventeenth century to take the overflow of Poor Clare sisters from its increasingly successful mother foundation at nearby Villemagne. The nuns were chased out by

the French Revolution less than two centuries later, since when it has been, among other things, a school, a hiding place for members of the Resistance during the Second World War, and a tenement building for the needy. Garrigae has simply provided new garb for a long-standing vocation.

Fabrice's guiding principle is the Native American proverb: 'We do not inherit the earth from our ancestors, we borrow it from our children'. He is impressed by the awareness of eco-values in this area north of the River Hérault and takes great care over his wine suppliers. "Nearly all my wines come from nearby vineyards and the organic quality is improving every year. One bio-dynamic grower even makes his own essential oil of rosemary for treating his vines."

The table d'hôtes dinner beneath the vault of the old kitchen is a convivial, candlelit opportunity to taste the slow-cooked dishes of the local caterer who specialises in traditional recipes such as coq au vin and cassoulet; he also provides the charcuterie for the tempting breakfast buffet. Salads, fresh vegetables and flowers come from a garden in the village. Next morning, you can fill your breakfast tray and take it to the garden, the pool, your suite –

wherever. "Guests should feel they are as free here as they are at home, says Fabrice."

"This is an area that visitors can explore with little outlay and much reward," he concludes. "The stunning gorges of the little Héric river are just down the road, the walks in the woods and hills of the regional nature park behind us are some of the finest, the lovely Lake Salagou is no distance for swimming and sailing and the sea is but a short drive." To return to a wine-tasting in the womb-like bar could be almost more pleasure than most of us can handle.

Fabrice Delprat

Le Couvent d'Hérépian, 2 rue du Couvent,
34600 Hérépian
- 13 suites: 11 for 2, 1 for 4 (double + twin). All with kitchen, sitting and dining spaces. €120-€355.
- Breakfast €13. Dinner from €20. Wines from €7.
- +33 (0)4 67 23 36 30
- www.garrigaeresorts.com
- Train station: Bédarieux

Villelongue Côté Jardins

AUDE

The lovely Claude and Renée are sisters, deeply rooted at Villelongue, green and slow in all they do, warm, knowledgeable and generous. This is where they were born. Then Claude went to marry and be an accountant in Toulouse while Renée became a teacher and stayed at home to look after their father. Now retired, they receive visitors in quiet wisdom, thriving on music and books, rich nature and good conversation with guests – and the absence of television.

They don't travel much but they do take the 'Courrier International' weekly to keep up with foreign affairs, understand their visitors and feed the talk at dinner: they are interesting and lively conversationalists. "The time we spend with people is worth every minute; they all have different opinions and it can get very exciting. Breakfast needs time, too. Sometimes we have to shoo our guests out at midday to go and do their 'job' as tourists while we deal with the house."

Villelongue is a group of seventeenth-century buildings on medieval foundations set round a great open courtyard garden, all part of the twelfth-century Cistercian abbey whose ruined church looms beyond. The monastic estate was sold off in bits after the French Revolution had confiscated all church property in 1789. The Marcoul family bought the former abbot's house and stables in 1938, becoming the fourth owners since the church was evicted one and a half centuries earlier.

History and romance combine in the long old house where dark passages and uneven stone floors lead into big beamed rooms that are pure 'French trad'. Renée and Claude choose to live with what they have; there is nothing exotic or smart and it is unashamedly dated, with enormous atmosphere. Claude's artistic eye for the stylishly sober is especially visible in the two most recently renovated rooms.

Animals wild and tame share the sisters' piece of deep countryside. They know every tree, flower, duck and roaming cat (some ancient, all neutered). Their two friendly dogs go everywhere with them, particularly enjoying Renée's expeditions into the woods to gather mushrooms and wild asparagus. "I also bring back old bottles and tins left by careless walkers." The dogs won't go across the river to the marsh where the wild boar live, though. "Those are pretty rough beasts," says Claude. "They are partial to arum lily bulbs and the sows sometimes bring their young to raid the garden for a fast-food snack. They wreak total havoc but we don't get the hunters in with their guns; we just go by every day and replant the daffodil and cyclamen bulbs they have dug

up and rejected. We both of us dig, sow and weed the potager by hand, too, for a harvest of rich-tasting vegetables grown without those weedkillers or pesticides that poison the ground and the animals. Our ducks love slugs and snails and we use macerated nettles and horse manure to nurture the soil." The Cistercian hydraulic system that has supplied the abbey with water for eight centuries still provides for all Villelongue's watering needs.

Claude loves cooking, doing it all from scratch. "When I was an accountant, I was always in a hurry and never did any real cooking. Fortunately, I was 'downsized' by my firm in my mid-fifties and could come back to real life in Villelongue. It is out of the question now that we use any processed foods with all their additives. Our vegetables are organic,

> "Our ducks love slugs and snails and we use macerated nettles and horse manure to nurture the soil"

home-grown or from nearby market gardens, the meat is from three local butchers who take their own animals to slaughter and track every piece. I take all the time needed for each ingredient, mixing, marinading, simmering; it's sheer pleasure." With such attentive preparation, dinner in the creaky, friendly dining room is a feast for eyes, taste buds and mind.

Mirroring their lively owners, the two old Welsh ponies do not always take their retirement peacefully and will occasionally break through the fence to look for other food and a bit of excitement. In winter, the birds gather to feast on the balls of fat and seeds that Claude hangs in the bushes for them. "We watch them feed as we sit at our winter occupations. We always brush the dogs out in the field so the birds can gather their fur, as well as the ponies' horsehair, for their nests."

All the linen in this house is antique, found in Emmaus Community shops and brought home for the delicate repair work that Renée does painstakingly and beautifully when the days are shorter and visitors fewer. "Old lace curtains and a well-dressed table fit the age and atmosphere of our house. We make all our own jam, cooking it for hours so that it gels with minimum sugar and no gelling agents. Every morning, it's decanted from the preserving jars into the antique sugar bowls that we have picked up over the years."

A painter's or a poet's paradise, this is a magical place to stay and commune with nature, or explore the vast cultural riches of the area – Carcassonne is twenty minutes, the Canal du Midi half an hour – and come home to dine with women of rare value and humanity. "Of course we eat with our guests, these are irreplaceable opportunities for astonishing contacts."

Villelongue is an inspiration to seekers of genuine human companionship and slow, authentic ways of living.

Claude Antoine & Renée Marcoul

Villelongue Côté Jardins,
11170 St Martin le Vieil
- 3: 1 double, 1 twin, 1 family room for 3.
- €60.
- Dinner with wine, €22, except July/August.
- +33 (0)4 68 76 09 03
- www.avillelongue.free.fr
- Train station: Carcassonne

L'Orri de Planès

PYRÉNÉES-ORIENTALES

Come by train, get off at the Planès request stop, walk fifteen minutes up through the forest to the lodge, and you will be given a ten percent discount. A hundred years ago the Train Jaune was created to connect the Roussillon coast to the high plateaux of the eastern Pyrenees and open up the remote mountain settlements. It was electric from the start and several hydro-electric stations were built near the line simply to service it. The executioner's axe has been raised more than once but this, the highest railway line in France, has survived to carry 400,000 tourists every year, winding along the hillsides. It is the perfect way for body and spirit to arrive at L'Orri de Planès.

Environmentalists to the tips of their toes, eco-warriors in a stunningly beautiful battlefield, Arif, architect and English teacher, and Marta, translator and Catalan teacher, are now demonstrating practical eco-respect. They lived in buzzy Barcelona which they loved – but they loved the mountains and the snow even more. Unhappy with the steady march of insatiable consumerism and its destruction of the planet, they let the idea of settling in the Pyrenees germinate slowly. When they decided to act, they chose the French side of the range because of its natural richness, low-key economy and wonderful skiing, particularly for Marta's speciality, cross-country skiing. So here they are, 1600 metres up, running and developing their eco-lodge for hikers, skiers and riders, campers and B&B adventurers.

An 'orri' is a traditional stone shepherd's hut built as a remote refuge for use during the long high-plateau grazing season. Arif and Marta chose the name to emphasise their solidarity with those who live and work in the mountains. Sustainability has guided their renovation and extension of the old Pyrenean stone barn. They chose a thermal system to regulate temperature using very little fuel; solar

systems which heat the water and produce enough electricity to cover most of their needs; and recycling to minimise rubbish. They have put sweat, blood and passion into building the place, where they live with two faithful mountain dogs and two cats, Rampell, a full tom who rampages through the neighbourhood, and Noisette, a pretty, delicate home-cat.

These wonderful people have four passions: the mountains ("and the mountains, and the mountains," says Marta), welcoming guests to the Orri, their animals – and "our secret weapon: conviviality." Dinner in the powerful atmosphere of the double-height dining room, with everyone at three big solid wooden tables round a single menu, brings people together for what she calls "the great French tradition of home cooking." Arif and Marta often eat with their guests and will gladly talk about the sourcing of their delicious foods.

From here, you look north to France, south to Spain. The Cardagne plateau – with more wildflowers and butterflies than most of us can ever dream of – supports cows, sheep and goats, giving three types of milk, cheese and yogurt. Fruit and vegetables come from two organic farms in the Prades valley, one of them run by a Senegalese woman who makes her own sorbets. Marta is a spontaneous cook, adapting her menus to whatever she receives from these local suppliers. The season up here is too short to grow their own but nothing served at the Orri comes from a supermarket.

"We are surrounded by mountain pastures and we have easy access to excellent meat but I don't do meat every day. I regularly plan vegetarian meals, and I include plenty of fresh seasonal fruit and vegetables in every menu." One of her favourite recipes is Escalivade Catalane, a deeply satisfying dish of Mediterranean vegetables marinaded in olive oil and cooked over charcoal embers. "Orri meals are served family style: I put the dishes on the table and encourage guests to eat as much as they like. At the same time, I try to instil an appreciation of the inherent value of what we serve. Most guests understand this and, as a result,

very little food is wasted." Packaging must be minimal, too, and recycling is a priority.

The lodge is furnished in the same spirit: no frills, just vast wooden beams, terracotta floors, stone walls and a Norwegian wood-burning stove. Small, spotless bedrooms and bathrooms are simple – 'less is more' is the motto – and decoration is kept to a minimum. Natural materials have their own sensuality, bright colours make it fun. What need for designer flourishes when nature provides a permanent slideshow outside, the sky changing every hour and wildflowers marching up to the door? After creating the inn and restaurant and the collective gîte for eighteen, Arif and Marta have just finished their 'Moon Camp', a terrace above the refuge with four luminous little yurts. And there's a secret spot down by the stream for those who want a meditative night.

Just up the road, past the fromagerie run by the shepherd, there's a tiny listed eleventh-century church, parapenters hovering silently overhead. The Trans-Pyrenees hiking trail (GR10) passes the door and three hundred metres above the Orri is the spectacular, secret Planès valley. Further north beyond the ramparts of Mont Louis, is Lake Matemale with sailing and windsurfing.

But it hasn't all been easy: "This medieval fiefdom, the kingdom of Planès, is mired in resistance and suspicion," says Arif. "Out there is France: another planet is how the townspeople see it. Eco-philosophy is beyond them for the moment; they have a slash and burn mentality. We are the only inn up here promoting local producers. Let's hope our example will change things."

Arif Qureshi & Marta Maristany

L'Orri de Planès, Cases del Mitg, 66210 Planès
- 10: 1 family room for 4; 4 doubles, 4 twins, sharing 4 baths; dorm for 6-8 with bath, shower & kitchen.
- €30 p.p. Children €25. Half board €50 p.p; children €35.
- Dinner with wine, €20. Children €10.
- +33 (0)4 68 04 29 47
- www.orrideplanes.com
- Train station: Planès or Perpignan

Can Llouquette

PYRÉNÉES-ORIENTALES

Full many a glorious morning have I seen
Flatter the mountain-tops with sovereign eye,
Kissing with golden face the meadows green,
Gilding pale streams with heavenly alchemy.
Shakespeare
Sonnet 33

"Sometimes the wilderness here in north Catalonia feels like the Great Rift Valley of East Africa where I grew up," says Simon, "and the 'false acacia' trees look like the acacias of the African grasslands. After three years, I am improving my French and Spanish, learning a few words of Catalan and feeling thoroughly at home in Montferrer." The ever-present Pyrenees have shaped the way of life in this, the southernmost valley in France, although there is seldom any lasting snow at this altitude. The stream that rushes down the hill to feed Can Llouquette, an old apple farm, never dries up. The terrain is so twisted and stony that it can only support less than one cow per hectare and has to be terraced for the slightest human project. "When our house was built two or three hundred years ago, they simply carved a platform out of the hillside and used the schist rocks to build these eighty-centimetre-thick walls, taking trees from the hillside to make the roof and adding sills and lintels of local granite."

He and Ashley, an opera singer, came here "to change our outlook on life and have more time for the things that matter – family, friends and life balance – and to Go Slow well before retiring. We haven't yet managed that last bit, I have to say, there's too much to do, but we spend all our time together as a family (our daughter Sophia was born in 2008) and that makes such a difference." Ashley, having spent two years turning the old house into a home, tending husband, baby, gîte guests and

walking groups, and adapting to her new life up a mountain (they lived in Edinburgh before coming here), is laying the ground for a gradual return to the music festival and recital circuit.

For Simon, clearing the land, improving the house and the gîte for visitors, making a separate office cabin for his website and marketing business, creating a vegetable plot and fencing the land for animals have been huge jobs in this rocky terrain

> "We have our own spring, solar hot water, our own timber for central heating, and electricity from the village's hydro-electric plant"

with its forty percent slope. The one raised vegetable bed produced all the salad ingredients they needed last summer so he is installing a further ten on one of the ledge-like terraces. That's the kind of man he is. The fencing posts are made with chestnut poles from Can Llouquette land or

harvested in the woods above it, in partnership with the woodman. Once the fences are finished, Ashley and Simon plan to bring in goats and sheep to help manage their hectares and find a companion for Zouky the lovable rescue donkey.

The family's participation in the local community was gradual, until 2009 propelled Simon to television fame and the status of local hero. In January, a violent storm swept through the valley, bringing down telephone poles and cutting the distant hamlets off from the world. By August the cries of the scattered subscribers had still not been heard, so our web-savvy Scotsman joined forces with the mayor of Montferrer, mounted his shining white charger (the faithful Zouky) and created the 'disgruntled donkey' website to carry the cause (petitanemecontent.org). This quickly attracted the attention of the local media. The day after the interview was broadcast, three repair teams were up the mountain, within a week every far-flung house had been reconnected and the telephone company was covered in shame. Shortly afterwards, when Ashley took Sophia down to the crèche they were greeted with affection and gratitude by the locals.

"Remarkably for so small a village," she says, "Montferrer has a restaurant serving lunch and dinner – they only close if no customers turn up – and a communal bakery-cum-café. This pivot of the community is owned by the council and run by a wonderful woman brimming with verve and commitment." Simon is negotiating with the mayor for the town hall's internet connection to be available on WiFi inside the café so that disadvantaged citizens – the poorer, the older, the less techno-competent – can use the web.

"We work with stunning nature at every vista: boundless butterflies and flowers, the sound of the river, the birds, the wind in the trees. We have our own spring, solar hot water, our own timber for central heating, and electricity from the village's hydro-electric plant. We now plan to adapt the centuries-old not-quite-ruined aqueduct system to create a big enough head of water for our own small generating turbine."

Meanwhile, rare lammergeier (the vividly-named 'bone-breaker') and griffon vultures wheel overhead, shy polecats hide in the thick woods and at night one can hear the wild boar making what

Simon describes as "a demonic noise" as they overturn rocks down by the stream.

"Our evenings with guests round the dinner table have produced some memorable and far-reaching conversations with exceptional people. Moving here was almost like turning our backs on the urban world. Now, opening our house to visitors is bringing the world back in – but on our own terms and, we hope, taking us towards a slower, more measured and meaningful existence. We see ourselves as guardians of Can Llouquette, not owners."

Simon Williams & Ashley Barrington

Can Llouquette - Bergerie & Studio, 66150 Montferrer
- Bergerie: 1 double, 1 twin. Studio: 1 double.
- Bergerie £350-£850, studio £175-£420, per week. Linen €20 p.p.
- Dinner, with wine, €18. Restaurant 3km.
- +33 (0)4 68 89 16 64
- www.can-llouquette.com
- Train station: Perpignan

[PROVENCE - ALPS - RIVIERA]

[PROVENCE - ALPS - RIVIERA]

Provençal cooking is based on garlic. The air in Provence is impregnated with the aroma of garlic, which makes it very healthful to breathe. Garlic is the main seasoning in bouillabaisse and in the principal sauces of the region. The lower classes in Provence often lunch on a crust of break sprinkled with oil and rubbed with garlic.
Alexandre Dumas Grand Dictionnaire de Cuisine

The people of Provence are renowned for their 'gastronomy of the sun'. Understandably, since the ingredients grow at their feet. Wild garlic and fennel can be foraged in the hedgerows; line upon line of olive trees produce rich olives and oils; herbs – thyme, oregano, sarriette, rosemary, fennel – reveal themselves in aromatic clouds as you walk the hillsides; local vegetables – tomatoes, peppers, aubergines, courgettes - gorge themselves on sunlight and heat. The food is alive with colour, generosity and invitations to pleasure. Cézanne loved simple food and when asked what his favourite dish was, he would reply "potatoes in oil."

Vines grew here even before the Romans came to improve the grapes for wine and table, and goats were sources of meat and milk. (It is rumoured that Roman Emperor Antoninus Pius died of a surfeit of Banon goat's cheese.) Because pollution and over-fishing are destroying stocks, the Mediterranean has trouble nowadays providing for a full *bouillabaisse à la Dumas* but a delicious Provençal fish soup can be made with unthreatened species – and lots of garlic.

The Provençal poet Mistral said "When the good lord has doubts about the world, he remembers that he created Provence." It is no surprise that this paradise on earth is a microcosm of the history of Europe: everyone wanted a share of the beautiful land and its resources, especially the flat bits near the sea. Marseille was founded by Greek merchants in the seventh century BC and has two fossilised ships to show for it. The Romans' first province in Gaul was Provence; they spread far and wide and stayed for six centuries, leaving temples, arches and, at Orange, one of the finest Roman amphitheatres. The fourteenth century saw a peculiar quirk of history when seven Popes ruled the church from Avignon for seventy years, to be followed by two anti-popes.

Where the hills begin to rise towards the less hospitable Alps, the people lived as they still do in the spaces available among the steep-sided valleys, volcanic domes and narrow basins of this powerful landscape. They fortified their villages, some on hilltop perches, against barbarians and feudal opponents. Here too, in wooded solitude, the Cistercian monks of the twelfth century built the 'three sisters,' the lovely abbeys of Le Thoronet, Sénanque and Silvacane, their frugal architecture and atmosphere in strong contrast to the wealthy towns and beaches of the plains.

Modern artists have been drawn to the light and landscapes of Provence; their works inform the popular image of the region: Cézanne painted his beloved Montagne Sainte Victoire dozens of times, Van Gogh's fields and sunflowers shimmer on many a dining-room wall. Provence today is a dynamic combination of tradition and modernity, tourism and the IT business. Nature parks encourage responsible tourism and high-level festivals attract the great names in music, theatre and dance.

[PROVENCE – ALPS – RIVIERA]

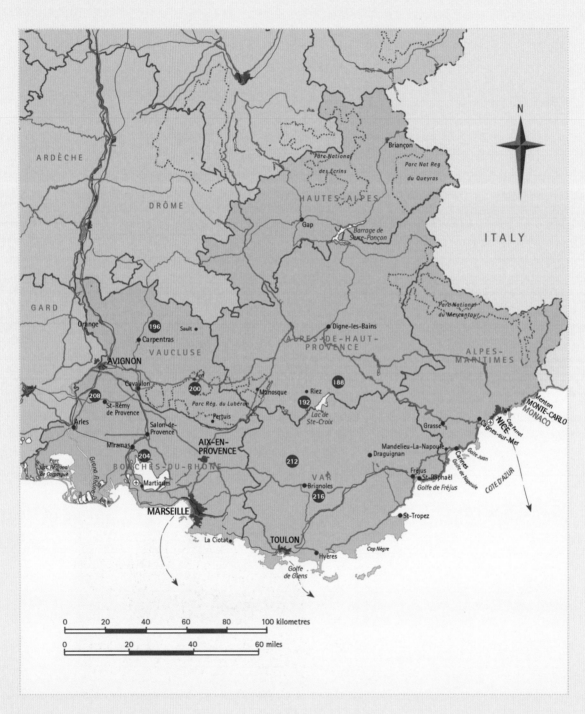

Special places to stay

Provence

Ferme de Félines

PROVENCE – ALPS – RIVIERA

"Going down the steep, unsurfaced, mountain-side road with vultures wheeling overhead, you could be forgiven for wishing yourself elsewhere. On leaving, you will wish you were staying. The view from the bedroom alone is worth it. So are Félines and Rita, they are unique." This visitor's words need little explaining, just look at the picture. The view plunges down the hill, over the truffle oaks, into the Lac de Sainte-Croix. The rest is a Provençal drama with Belgian roots.

"I have been Slow all my life," says Rita. "As a wild Belgian child, I used to say 'The day I can't dream here any longer, I'll go and dream elsewhere'. My inspirations were Kipling's Mowgli and Saint-Exupéry's Petit Prince. Today, I am pained by the obsessive materialism and dreadful waste of our times. Nothing is wasted in nature, everything is recycled in pursuit of The Project, which is life on earth. When the gardens of Belgium became concrete, the springs disappeared and the town invaded the countryside, I knew I could no longer live in my native country." Rita held firmly in her mind the vision of the wild, unspoilt place where she would land. When her children were able to fly solo, she found her vision in the Verdon valley. "Félines had all the ingredients: mountains, water, woods, pastures, a few rare species needing protection and practically no predators – apart from man. I knew I wanted to live here, I didn't know I would be joining Manon des Sources*."

The original farm was in ruins, having been plundered for its stones, beams and tiles and abandoned for twenty years. The many hectares of truffle orchard were in poor condition but the harvest of 'black diamonds', as truffles are known, had not been neglected by canny locals all those years. Rita planned a new bio-climatic house, "one that wouldn't pollute in its building or its running: no concrete, a timber frame made with trees felled by the gales,

renewable energy sources. My whole plan was refused because this is a listed area of outstanding natural beauty! So the house is made of concrete and heated with oil. At least I have water from a spring, the only one of the original three that hasn't dried up. Nine

> "I have been Slow all my life," says Rita. "As a wild Belgian child, I used to say 'The day I can't dream here any longer, I'll go and dream elsewhere'. My inspirations were Kipling's Mowgli and Saint-Exupéry's Petit Prince"

hundred metres from the house, it runs all year – except for the annual 'break-in' when the plumbing connections are stolen." She tries to get city-dwellers to realise the crucial importance of water and environmental protection but finds it hard persuading the younger generations who have never known shortages or frugality. "I tell them about the thirty

tons of rubbish cleared from the Verdon canyon in 2006, the open-air dumps that still ruin certain spots of surpassing beauty, perpetuated by thoughtless citizens and office-bound authorities."

With only enough water for her domestic needs, Rita can no longer grow vegetables or irrigate the four hundred replanted truffle oaks that still stand, while the prevailing drought means little natural watering and diminishing harvests. A tremendous walker still, she goes down to the orchards with her two rescue dogs, survivors of a malicious poison attack when she left them for a few hours. She has trained them to hunt for truffles and they love their winter expeditions – truffles ripen between November and March – though they don't scare the poachers. "The days leading up to full moon are the most productive," says Rita, "and we watch for signs of wildlife as we go, the remaining deer, hares, red partridges and, of course, wild boar; this year, for the first time, I saw three pheasants."

Although the truffle cannot be cultivated anyway, she has had the whole estate certified organic to make a statement to her contemporaries and hand on something of lasting value. She now hopes to find a beekeeper willing to put hives on her land. "There are

quantities of wild thyme on my hillsides and honey from wild thyme is sheer magic for healing wounds." She buys organic and local and is no stranger to special diets; there are always non-dairy products and gluten-free bread as well as local eggs and charcuterie, fruit, fresh juice and homemade smoothies on her generous breakfast table. Easygoing to a fault, she even encourages guests to make a picnic for their day's hiking.

Rita does not advertise dinners, nor does she organise anything formally, but an *aperitif provençal* can easily turn into an evening round the barbecue "with a free-range chicken brought unexpectedly by the farmer and whatever the rest of the company brings in the way of food for body, and for mind: ideas, inspiration, poetry."

"Mine is the most beautiful spot in the Verdon," says Rita, with conviction. "I have decorated and furnished the house soberly so that nature's beauty holds centre stage, but at seven kilometres from the village it comes at a price. I am at the end of the line and the first to have my electricity, telephone and internet cut off. I choose to live as a semi-hermit a lot of the time and hugely enjoy my fellow creatures when they come to share Félines with me. I know a

few people nearby who build their lives on similar ideas to mine and I've recently met a member of the National Hunting and Wildlife Commission whose job is to hunt the poachers. All animals, from insect to elephant, are my friends while the humans who find their way to my door bring other rewards; we recharge each other's batteries. I have met some remarkable people doing B&B." Her wine glasses are engraved with 'Carpe Diem'.

* Marcel Pagnol's sequel to "Jean de Florette", a tragic tale, set in the Cévennes, of water feud and greed in a claustrophobic village.

Rita Ravez

Ferme de Félines, Route des Gorges du Verdon, 04360 Moustiers Ste Marie
- 3 doubles.
- €125.
- Restaurants in Moustiers.
- +33 (0)4 92 74 64 19
- www.ferme-de-felines.com
- Train station: Aix en Provence

Le Moulin du Château

PROVENCE - ALPS - RIVIERA

This place ticks all the boxes. A glorious setting, a château looking benignly down over the fence, a site inside the Verdon regional nature park*, poppies among the stones, a Slow Food mindset, bikes for guests – and battalions of birds. The Moulin du Château is a bird sanctuary and one of the country's twenty-one Hôtels au Naturel*. Sited in a nature park, these sign a charter undertaking to offer solid knowledge of their park, its birds, plants and ecosystems, and to work to reduce their eco-footprint. At this particular Hôtel au Naturel, they go the extra mile, singing the virtues of sustainable tourism to locals and visitors alike. "At the same time," adds Nicolas, "it's interesting to see that the smaller farms around here are gradually converting to organic methods, mostly at the hands of 'outsiders'."

Nicolas and Edith, who are a mixture of Swiss, French and Italian, joined Slow Food Switzerland when they were teachers there and have been ardent followers of the organic movement for years. They wanted to live in France but had no idea that they would one day be running a hotel and cooking for others. "We had planned to open a language school," says Nicolas, "but discovered we'd had enough of teaching. This life suits us perfectly. It is really hard work for

eight months of the year yet we find it tremendously rewarding. We're living in a corner of paradise, doing things we enjoy, making friends from all over the world and promoting local artists." Nicolas' daughter lives nearby and he has four grandchildren. Children are, naturally, welcome at the Moulin where they find an instant playmate in Lila the bouncy young collie. "She herds the two cats as if they were sheep – and the clients, too."

Edith and Nicolas alternate as cooks and waiters, with a couple of local assistants who have been here since the beginning. It's a point of pride with them that no guest is served the same dish twice and they both have an anthology of over sixty recipes to choose from. Edith especially enjoys cooking vegetables, revelling in what these Mediterranean lands produce. "In Provence, good food is taught at mother's knee, family traditions of growing and cooking one's own food still exist and our tomatoes – gathered ripe and taken straight to the table – are out of this world. There's great variety and a lot of organic produce down here. You can find us out in the woods occasionally, foraging for wild asparagus, garlic and leeks. Then there's our unique free-range goat's cheese, the Banon, the only one with the coveted AOC label, its aromatic

Menu 30 août 2009

Salade de carottes à l'orange
Magret de canard fumé

Poulet fumé au sésame
sur un lit d'épeautre
Poivrons aux amandes

Fromage fermier

Fraises du pays au sorbet de fraise

creaminess wrapped in chestnut leaves... people take them home by the boxful."

The mill, built almost four hundred years ago to press the château's olives, served its purpose until the 1950s. The original donkey-powered press, still here in all its stoney massiveness, is the focus of the living room, next to the billiard table. Everywhere, thick stone walls, arches and changes in level bear witness to the long story of the building but Edith and Nicolas have fitted their very simple furniture into the old frame without pushing or overpowering. "We haven't built a swimming pool either, and the outdoor shower is solar-powered. The Verdon river, named for the clear greenness of its water and with the deepest canyon in Europe, has plenty of places just inviting you to take a dip 'au naturel'. Our only air conditioning is natural, too, thanks to these thick stone walls and shutters."

One of Nicolas' sculptures marches through the garden but he finds he doesn't get time to be an artist as well as hotel keeper and restaurateur. Instead, as a way of filling their empty walls and financing contemporary art, he and Edith have founded an association to show the works of local artists in the hotel and manage an annual sale. "Our clients are as interested in the works as they are in our eco-friendly attitudes. We don't preach but we do leave them notes about the organic movement and price lists for the art. They often ask us for more details and buy organic oil or jam or honey from our shop. We feel we are making good progress."

And then there are the birds, many and varied. Fifteen years of chemical-free sanctuary among the trees, shrubberies and hedgerows have not gone unnoticed. A colony of over a hundred sparrows has taken up permanent residence, the house martins hunt in great whistling swoops every summer's evening, the 'petit duc' (scops owl) is heard in the garden at night – "what's that alarm?" someone may say at the sound of its monotonous repetitive call – and the nightingale has been known to sing from dusk to dawn. "We have robins and tits and

hoopoes. Other nature-lovers have been re-introducing griffon vultures into the gorges, with great success, and there are eagles out there, and gulls and cormorants." It's a bird-lovers' dream where rock-climbers may find themselves face to face with a ten-foot vulture.

"This is a place of complete rest where people come to escape the agitation of modern life, to contemplate the fabulous wild landscapes and enjoy that rarity, a natural holiday." Some say they feel they've stepped back forty years to the pre-electronic age – and that includes the spectacular boat trip down the Gorges du Verdon. "Yes, life here is rich and good and as earth-friendly as we can make it – what more could we want?"

* National & Regional Nature Parks and Hôtels au Naturel - see p. 248.

see p. 248.

Edith & Nicolas Stämpfli-Faoro

Le Moulin du Château, 04500 Saint Laurent du Verdon
- 10: 5 doubles, 2 twins, 1 triple, 1 quadruple, 1 suite.
- €105-€137. Half-board €165-€197 for 2.
- Breakfast €9. Picnic lunch €10. Dinner €30 (except Mon & Thurs). Wine €6-€30. Restaurants nearby.
- +33 (0)4 92 74 02 47
- www.moulin-du-chateau.com
- Train station: Aix en Provence

Château Juvenal

PROVENCE - ALPS - RIVIERA

A fairytale for our time? In Grenoble, called the Silicon Valley of France, a high-powered couple in a high-tech industry decide, before they are fifty, to turn their backs on the excitement of jet-setting success. They 'retire' to the country and a new activity that won't bubble and burst, a life where they can bring up Eva, their late-born daughter, themselves rather than losing her to baby-sitters. Ten years ago, Anne-Marie and Bernard found a sleeping beauty of a château deep in a romantic nineteenth-century Provençal park; it even had frogs in the ponds and midwife toads in the undergrowth. Using their well-honed project-management skills, they set about re-awakening its beauty under the age-old eyes of the spectacular Dentelles de Montmirail.

Standing among sweeps of terraced hillsides, shaded by superb old trees, the lovely house had been left to sleep for the proverbial hundred years.

There were vines and olive groves all around. Just what they wanted. They restored it from scratch, saving every ounce of its soul. Warped original windows were re-used as cupboard doors, original roof-insulating bricks relaid as floors, damaged beams supported on hand-crafted stone brackets, traditional paints and finishes applied. The furniture at Juvenal is properly antique, too, with some pieces that have made their way down three centuries or more.

Bernard and Anne-Marie then made two fine apartments in the old farmhouse next to the château, and now they are turning their energies to the estate. At present, the vines are cultivated by a talented young neighbour with minimal use of chemicals and the local winery turns the grapes into a well-reputed AOC Ventoux 'Château Juvenal'. In 2011, the operations will go organic and the two estates will join forces to make their own wine – a big step.

The new storage shed will carry photovoltaic cells for making electricity. Saving energy matters to Anne-Marie and Bernard, though it isn't always easy at Juvenal. This is Mistral country and the cold north wind blows so hard down the Rhône Valley in winter that they move out of the big high-ceilinged château into one of their wood-heated farmhouse apartments, receiving B&B guests in the other.

In the nineteenth century a local poet, the aptly-named Frédéric Mistral, launched a double campaign for Provençal independence (a lost cause in hyper-centralised France), and the dying Provençal Occitan language, now revived and even taught in some state schools. In one of the apartments, the Forestiers painted his portrait and his hymn to the light, the colours and the wine of their adopted country:

> Le soleil semble se coucher
> dans un verre de Tavel
> aux tons rubis irisés de topaze.
> Mais c'est pour mieux se lever dans les cœurs.
> (The sun seems to set
> in a glass of Tavel
> the colour of rubies iridescent with topaz,
> all the better to rise in our hearts.)

After forty years of fast living elsewhere and ten years of her new existence here, Anne-Marie says "I feel that the essential part of my life has been at Juvenal; this is where I have found meaning." When they first arrived, they were amazed at the slow pace of life and the attention people gave to others. "Like everyone everywhere, they said 'Good morning, how are you?' The difference was that they actually listened to your reply. A Provençal talks slowly, pronouncing all the vowels, taking time over the words and the relationship." Anne-Marie believes that she talks more slowly now, too. "My dream, all those years in the city, was to ride my own horse out into the countryside. With B&B guests half the year, I can't have my own horse but I ride when I can, with the wife of our organic fruit-juice producer: that's pretty close to the dream."

The best time of all, they say, is the olive harvest in November. No scientist has ever

managed to mechanise or control the olive tree's (or the truffle's) production. The climate and the *terroir** decide how many olives a tree will grow and the amount can vary by five hundred percent from year to year. Only manual gathering saves the fruit from damage during harvesting. "So we close for a week and invite family and friends to our *olivades* (olive festival) – or *amitiades* (friend festival) as we like to call it. And what a festival it is! We have a wonderful time doing this 'job'." Their olives, which have a naturally low acid content, are sent in batches of four hundred kilos to local mills where they are pressed separately, unblended and mostly within twenty-four hours. The result is a delicious pure-Juvenal extra-virgin oil.

Table d'hôtes evenings are important to the Forestiers. They share the cooking – organic and local fresh ingredients only – and dine with their guests at one big table, always. Their mastery of English often helps keep the conversation open to all. "We hope to give our guests a taste of the slow natural life of Château Juvenal. We explain everything they want to know about the area and what to do here over a welcome drink and a leisurely, healthy breakfast the next morning. Breakfast consists of homemade bread and preserves, cereals, cheese and plenty of fruit. And we hope to meet them again over dinner one evening during their stay."

Anne-Marie's summary of her days here is "I always have something to do but am never under pressure."

Anne-Marie & Bernard Forestier

Château Juvenal, Chemin du Long Serre,
84330 Saint Hippolyte le Graveyron
• 1 double, 2 twins/doubles, 1 suite for 2-3. 2 apts for 4-6.
• €110-€170. Apts €900-€1,600 per week.
• Hosted dinner with wine, €36, twice weekly.
• +33 (0)4 90 62 31 76
• www.chateau-juvenal.com
• Train station: Carpentras

Auberge du Presbytère

PROVENCE – ALPS – RIVIERA

Saignon is pure Provence, set against the rocky backdrop of the Grand Lubéron where walking takes you to aromatic heaven as you crush the wild thyme underfoot. The Mediterranean garrigue that hugs the dry slopes feels as old as the hills themselves. The Rocher de Saignon is a short and easy walk; from the ridge, on a clear day, the eye reaches across a heart-stopping panorama of waves set in stone, north to Mont Ventoux, east to the foothills of the Alps, a sea of beauty. Frédéric Mistral puts it with nineteenth-century flamboyance:

> *Sur la mer de l'histoire,*
> *pour moi, tu fus, ô ma Provence,*
> *un pur symbole, un mirage de*
> *gloire et de victoire qui,*
> *dans l'écoulement ténébreux*
> *des siècles,*
> *nous laisse voir un éclair de*
> *Beauté.*
> (For me, on the sea of history,
> oh my Provence, you were a
> pure symbol, a mirage of glory
> and victory that, in the stormy
> flow of the centuries, leaves a
> flash of beauty.)

Water runs in fountains and basins at every corner of this village. At the heart of the web of narrow streets, the Auberge du Presbytère unfolds onto a square whose carved stone fountain is fed by water flowing straight from the hills. This is where villagers, restaurant staff

and customers fill their water jugs. The Lubéron, too infertile to be cultivated, with only scattered cattle and sheep and no chemicals, filters the water to near-perfection.

The day Gerhard and Anne-Cécile first visited Saignon five years ago, the streets were full of children: it was carnival for Saignon's exceptionally young population. They knew instantly that this was a place that lived all year round, not a tourist museum that closed down in winter, and the children would find lasting friends. As Gerhard tells it: "Our son, then five, was pushing us to leave the filth and noise of Paris with its alienated people and no space to play. Now ten, he says he wants to help save giant turtles from extinction when he grows up. He's a born environmentalist and a great inspiration to us." Gerhard and Anne-Cécile, who now have three children, knew they needed to get out of the city and slow down. Gerhard was travelling too much as a business consultant and wanted to be his own boss. They both longed for clean air and a garden and a place where the children could play on their own without being hemmed in by safety barriers. "We now live in what one friend calls a 'slowed-down context' and I believe the current crisis is, of necessity, going to force our world into a slower, healthier way of life."

The inn is a patchwork of four stone houses from the seventeenth

and eighteenth centuries, sensitively but firmly restored by the Roses. They only changed what really needed changing. "We hate the idea of throwing things out just because someone else has used them. The tables and chairs in the restaurant came with the walls, we simply stripped and repainted them for their new life. I love this place. The bathrooms were done in the 1980s

> "They both longed for clean air and a garden and a place where the children could play on their own without being hemmed in by safety barriers"

with tiles from Apt that are not made any more, so we'll keep them – and they'll soon be valuable antiques!" Each room is a variation on a country-Provençal theme with a view from the window and no television. They are intended as places for quiet reading, rest and contemplation.

"All our renovations have been done with healthy, local materials such as wood and terracotta. We use lime renders coloured with Roussillon ochres; they have no resins or chemicals, keep germs and mould away, let the old walls breathe, and they last. Indeed, we wanted to keep the spirit of the previous owners alive: the first were a couple of 1968 health-and-nature seekers, the second a more conventional couple who aimed to keep things simple. I have always taken pleasure in having guests and, fortunately, in restoring old buildings. I even wanted to open a bar when I was young but people said that wasn't a serious career option... then. I think we have created a comfortable, welcoming place with no pretensions and luxury that doesn't shout."

The importance of detail stretches beyond the building and restaurant. "We use local suppliers and craftsmen wherever possible, the village cabinet-maker, potter and wrought-ironsmith, the chair-mender from the next village, the nearby

market gardeners and small farmers for our daily provisions. This area is rich in resources and there's no need to go for miles to shop. The chef takes his inspiration from the day's market, be it Cavaillon melon or Sisteron lamb, asparagus from Lauris (where the commercial variety was first developed) or Camargue bull's-meat, strawberries from Carpentras, and organic wine." Dining on the flowery terrace in summer or by the big open fireplace in winter is a gastronomic tour of the fruits and tastes of Provence.

The lovely twelfth-century church next door is listed, quite rightly, but there's an unfortunate side effect: permission to put solar panels on any part of the inn's many roofs has not yet been given. Gerhard reckons, however, that he will eventually be allowed to use the 'invisible' sides of his roofs. The auberge will still be a worthy part of the fabric of old Saignon while becoming a more eco-attentive member of the community.

Anne-Cécile & Gerhard Rose

Auberge du Presbytère,
Place de la Fontaine, 84400 Saignon
• 16 twins/doubles. €60-€145.
• Breakfast €10.50. Lunch & dinner €20-€38. Restaurant closed Wed.
• +33 (0)4 90 74 11 50
• www.auberge-presbytere.com
• Train station: Avignon

Mas de la Rabassière

PROVENCE – ALPS – RIVIERA

"The enemy is the telly," is Michael's declared opinion. "A meal is a marvellous time for talking and as the telly kills conversation, we keep ours in a dedicated room. Reading creates and is often created by conversation, so we have a large library, good reading lights on both sides of our beds, and... no telly in the bedrooms. A lot of our books are here because of conversations with guests." He is a live-wire host with stacks of experience and culture and a talent for getting the most cringing wallflower to relax.

Posted to France by a multinational, Michael fell in love with the country and retired to this untypically lush corner of Provence. He has been here for years, living in an olive grove of three hundred trees set in a quintessential Provençal landscape, with one corner that will be forever England: anyone for croquet in the rose garden? (Or swimming, or tennis, even.) Twenty years ago, the garden was a wilderness and the house a mish-mash of genuine old and insensitive new. Michael, a do-it-all-yourself man who loves using his hands, went to work, stopping from time to time to glory in the long view south across the low hills and vineyards to the Étang de Berre, one of the Mediterranean salt-water lagoons, the largest in Europe.

He rebuilt the house, often with local stone, always in local style,

with the help of a good local stonemason who did specialised things like columns, lintels and the drawing-room fireplace. He makes or repairs a lot of his own woodwork and has replaced most of the 'Parisian' shutters with his hand-made, traditional Provençal versions (the hinges are invisible when closed). He cleared the creepers and pine saplings that were choking the olive orchard and now harvests a fine crop from healthy trees. "It's good to see that many of my neighbours have followed suit in resuscitating their olive groves."

Music is as essential as books to Michael and Thevi, a gracious Tamil from Singapore who is his assistant and 'third daughter'. His much-loved old Blüthner grand piano is kept in tune and used for a handful of drawing-room concerts each year. Visitors professional and amateur are drawn to its lovely sound and impromptu recitals often delight the company. He subscribes to the Marseille Chamber Music Society and the region's many festivals, encouraging guests to join him with an offer of transport. "For the nearby Salon-de-Provence festival, one of the very best in Europe, I provide free lodging for two musicians; it's a marvellous week." Haydn or Mozart will waft you down to breakfast and homemade croissants each morning and La Rabassière's display of original art by guests and other friends. The bronzes are by a talented local sculptor, René Rovellotti, who welcomes guests into his studio; several have spent a creative week with him there.

Michael is an accomplished cook. "We offer proper Provençale cuisine, using large quantities of garlic and oil from our own olives. For many years I was an assiduous member of the Couqueto, a group of oldish ladies in Marseille with a mission to preserve and hand on good home cooking. That's what I want to do, too, and guests are always welcome in the kitchen. I think cooking can be a great social activity. Almost everything that is served here is homemade and wherever possible I buy local produce."

In this apparently studious, adult atmosphere, it is good to know that children are welcome at La Rabassière. "Children can take up a lot of time but

> "He rebuilt the house, often with local stone, always in local style, with the help of a good local stonemason who does specialised things like columns, lintels and the drawing-room fireplace"

it's time well spent. A friend horrified me recently by stating in a very matter-of-fact way that she preferred animals to children; I don't, and we don't allow pets in the house, but we encourage children of any age and seldom charge for them." Thevi has a grandchild who lives nearby. She deals deftly with things indoors and serves Michael's delicious dishes while her husband Bruno helps with the garden.

Garden waste goes onto the big compost heap that keeps the lushness alive. "A garden in Provence needs a lot of watering and we are extraordinarily lucky to have a gravity-fed canal bringing water from the Durance river in a sixteenth-century duct system. It uses almost no energy and gives us

virtually free water that would otherwise go straight into the sea."

The weather is balmy and mild in this part of the world so lunch at La Rabassière is served on the terrace almost every day of the year and one isn't aware of aeroplanes. For the brief spell when heating is needed, the ground-floor rooms, beautifully decorated in English country-house style with a few fine Provençal antiques, have open fireplaces. "We are surrounded by pine woods," says Michael. "They belong to our neighbour the local wine maker, whose wines I serve at meals (they are on tap throughout the day, too). Every winter we clear the fallen timber to improve the landscape, reduce the risk of fire and supply our own needs." The rest of the time, two sets of solar panels heat the water and power the reversible heat exchangers that cool the bedrooms in summer and heat them in winter.

A walk behind the house reveals the ancient dry-stone terracing that Michael has restored. Charming Saint Chamas has an even older Roman bridge to admire and a highly unusual eighteenth-century washing place, originally built for plague victims. This is a rich and fascinating region that deserves a slow visit. Michael, whose favourite town is Arles, has written the perfect information pack for guests.

Michael Frost

Mas de la Rabassière, 2137 chemin de la Rabassière, 13250 Saint Chamas

- 2 doubles.
- €135. Singles €85.
- Dinner with wine, €47.
- +33 (0)4 90 50 70 40
- www.rabassiere.com
- Train station: Aix en Provence

Mas de Cornud

PROVENCE - ALPS - RIVIERA

First, there is eternal Provence, the hillsides scented with wild herbs – rosemary, thyme, sage, lavender – and the rocky ridges of the low Alpilles range thrusting their bare greyness out of the green garrigue like the skeletons of prehistoric monsters. Powerful triumphal arches and elegant columns are reminders that the Romans, too, fell in love with this area two millennia ago. The air and soil at Mas de Cornud are as unpolluted as any in the south of France. The wooded hills and scrubland, however, scarcely lend themselves to farming, though it's ideal for goats and sheep, and there are few villages in the Alpilles proper. The quiet lowland country round Saint Rémy grows olives, fruits and vegetables, nothing intensive or over-chemical. The Mas stands beneath tall trees in fertile farmland just north of the foothills, the Canal des Alpilles feeds the lushness, local timber and home-cut prunings crackle in the open fireplaces and, as

David says, "the thick 200-year-old stone walls and traditional shutters are the air-conditioning plant."

Second, there is food, more food and other food. "Food is the focus of my life," says Nito, "this is where I have my Seasons of Provence Cooking School, the potager, the fig trees and my wonderful herb garden." Egyptian-born, she first learned to cook in Cairo, teaches Provençal and Middle Eastern cookery and belongs to an international forum to promote sustainable food. David, a well-travelled American, is the wine master, organising tastings at the Mas and taking any interested guests on vineyard tours. "We are long-standing and active members of the Provence chapter of Slow Food and source our ingredients with great care; as organic as possible, first from our own garden, the rest from farmers' markets, neighbouring farms and artisan suppliers." The kitchens, one indoors, one out, are superb. The

outdoor kitchen stretches to a wood-burning bread oven and a big open hearth with hand-cranked mechanical spit-roasting equipment, a replica of seventeenth-century methods.

One of Nito's first lessons is how to hold a knife to chop successfully. You can take a week-long or a one-day cookery course. "I guide people through the market and teach them to use their five senses to choose the best, ripest, most natural ingredients, what different oils smell and taste like, how to buy herbs by the bunch." She makes planning, buying and cooking feel like fun and her students love the convivial triumph of sharing their efforts with David and 'teacher' over the leisurely meal that always wraps up a cookery session. An extra feather in Nito's cap is an achievement for the Slow Food ethos: after one cookery lesson, taken out of curiosity rather than conviction (she was starting from scratch), a recent guest wrote to say she had converted to doing the cooking herself when she got back home instead of relying on processed meals.

Thirdly, both David and Nito love what they do and it shows. They laugh all the time, welcome guests like family and seem to be ever available to talk, explain and share. Graciously casual, they cook and serve and chat at table, be it dinner by moonlight on the terrace, lunch under the grape bower or in the delightful dining room. Children are happy here, curled up in the oriental corner of the salon (in honour of past lives in the Middle East and Turkey), swinging on the homemade swing, romping in the big garden with the endlessly playful Chépé, the rare Pharaoh hound named after Queen Chépénupet (first pictured in Egypt c. 4000 BC), and Maya the Chihuahua, recruited into the family during a cookery tour of Mexico.

"As well as suggesting vineyard tours," says David, "I encourage guests to walk in the wonderful landscape of the Alpilles. I have explored the area in depth and can recommend many hikes through the landscapes and light that inspired Van Gogh. Did you know he did over 150 paintings of the country around Saint Rémy?" Just five kilometres away, at the end of the little road that winds through the hills, is the amazing village of Les Baux that appears to grow straight out of the precipitous rock face. It's a fairly hard walk but worth it when you take the path; the arrival is far more dazzling than if you go by car."

Nito's galette de tomates aux olives noires de Provence
(Provençal tomato tart with black olives)

Serves 4
2 large onions, sliced
4 tbsp olive oil
1 tbsp caster sugar
2 tbsp water
1 puff pastry case – about 20cm in diameter
2 cloves garlic, chopped
Bunch of basil, shredded – reserve 10 tips for garnish
Salt & pepper
600g firm, ripe tomatoes, sliced 7mm thick
8 black olives
1 tbsp balsamic or Jerez vinegar
2 pinches fleur de sel salt

• Heat 2 tbsp olive oil in pot, sweat onions 2-3 mins
• Add sugar, salt, pepper, water. Toss, cover, lower
heat & simmer 20 mins or until of compote
consistency, stirring occasionally
• Precook pastry between oven trays covered with
greaseproof paper for 12 mins or until lightly coloured.

• Spread onion pastry to within 0.5 cm of edge.
Sprinkle with garlic & shredded basil
• Lay tomatoes to overlap
• Salt & pepper to taste, drizzle 1 tbsp olive oil
• Bake 10 mins in preheated oven until tomatoes
start to soften
• Remove from oven, garnish with olives & basil tips,
drizzle remaining oil & vinegar, sprinkle with fleur de
sel salt, serve hot

David & Nitockrees Tadros Carpita

Mas de Cornud, Petite Route des Baux (D31),
13210 Saint Rémy de Provence
• 6: 5 doubles, 1 suite for 2-5.
• €155–€250. Suite €240–€395.
• Picnic €40. Lunch €40–€50. Dinner with wine, €55–€65.
• +33 (0)4 90 92 39 32
• www.mascornud.com
• Train station: Avignon

Une Campagne en Provence

PROVENCE - ALPS - RIVIERA

These people live and breathe sustainability on their one hundred and seventy hectares of glorious Provençal countryside – ground-hugging garrigue and umbrella pines, Mediterranean scents and lavender blue – and the house, which from the cliff looks like a cottage and from the valley like a fortress, displays all the idiosyncrasies of its long history. In the twelfth century, the Templars built a 'commandery' farm up against this rock face, a system of irrigation channels that delivers water to this day, and a pigeon tower. Their bread oven was at ground level, the pigeons above it, the humans a floor higher, each gathering heat from below. After many adaptations, the place was given a 'bourgeois' makeover two hundred years ago and modernised with fireplaces and honeycomb tiles.

In the 1990s, Martina, from Germany, managed projects for a big chemicals multinational and Claude, who is French, was in charge of keeping the firm in the front line of environmental responsibility, a job that later took him to the World Business Council for Sustainable Development. When Fabrice was born, Martina decided to move to the farm they had started renovating and they set out to create a super-eco-friendly family home and guest house in this wonderful place. "It had always been a community," say Claude and Martina, "and that was what we wanted."

It's a long slow drive through forest, pastures and parkland before reaching the house at the heart of the estate. Not being farmers, what were they to do with the land? Claude devised a partnership scheme. Partners pay no rent but undertake to respect the Fusslers' rules and do things ecologically and prettily. The land is now used, tended and embellished by: a local sheep farmer whose four-hundred-strong flock roams wide and whose sheep especially like the sheltered woodland grazing; fourteen donkeys; the revived saffron beds (a fragile and highly specialised crop); a dozen livery and breeding horses stabled and

pastured here; the old vineyard, now thriving again; the shooting syndicate with whom it is agreed that two members act as gamekeepers so there will be no poaching, one area is totally no-shoot, bio-diversity is preserved and they keep a close eye on the woods.

"Everyone's happy with the arrangement," says Claude. "We have excellent relationships with our tenants, we are guaranteed beautiful, sustainably-managed hectares on our estate, children love the animals and adults enjoy the bucolic walks." "As well as the pretty Provençal bedrooms," adds Martina.

A wander through the garden reveals many surprises: you find corners for writing private letters, statues and carvings, water spouting and chuckling and lying still in the quiet light, dogs, cats and flocks of fowl. All the water used rises from Peyrourier's springs and wells and the virtuous cycle they have installed is a model of de-greaser, septic tank, earth filter and reed bed systems. "Nothing is lost," is Claude's comment. Since May 2009, they have had their own power station, too – a vast photovoltaic roof that also serves as an open shed for the wood pile – and they sell the power to the grid.

When the Fusslers planned their renovations, the architect was told: "There will be no fossil fuels on this estate, except one car and a tractor. No air conditioning, either." That car, by the way, is small and they won't change it "until there's an electric car available with proper servicing within twenty kilometres." The insulation is of Swiss-Alp quality and the house is heated by heat pumps and a fine traditional ceramic stove fed with fallen timber from their woods. The place has Provençal simplicity, great character and outstanding comfort.

To offset emissions, the estate is a pilot project for the NGO that plants slow-growing local species such as walnut, alder, mountain ash and wild cherry trees, managing them as carbon sinks and for cabinet-making. Claude has set up an information kiosk where the public can learn the principles and practices of carbon sinks. "We have some remarkable old trees in our woods, too, and always encourage guests to explore the remains of Provence's rural past there, on foot or on horseback. There are ruins of sheepfolds,

charcoal ovens (the last one only closed in the 1950s) and a lime kiln, all built with dry-stone walls, fascinating insights into how people made a living."

And dinner, after all that? It is a joyous, convivial, polyglot occasion where over twenty people may be gathered round several tables beneath the spreading plane trees, including one for Fabrice and visiting children. "The dishes are on the table as for a normal family meal," says Martina, "and we eat with our guests." She and her cook like making Mediterranean dishes with ingredients chosen from the market gardener's beds down by the river. "Our land is not ideal for growing vegetables but he grows lots, and he plants the things we like cooking; it's another perfect arrangement." Meat is generally local lamb or poultry with the occasional cut of wild boar and the whole thing is rounded off with a homemade fig or walnut liqueur.

This is a place with dedicated owners and environmental virtue, a paradise for children, wildlife and all its free-range domestic beasts.

Martina & Claude Fussler

Une Campagne en Provence,
Domaine le Peyrourier, 83149 Bras
- 5: 3 doubles, 1 suite, 1 studio for 2 with kitchenette.
- €95–€115. Suite €110–€120. Studio €110–€130.
- Hosted dinner with wine, €33. Restaurant 7km.
- +33 (0)4 98 05 10 20
- www.provence4u.com
- Train station: Aix en Provence

La Maison de Rocbaron

PROVENCE - ALPS - RIVIERA

Jeanne is a perfectionist – "I simply have to be alone when I'm cooking" – with a weakness for pink and an unusual story. She is one of those rare migrating birds, a Luxembourgeoise born and bred who left her country. Tiny Luxembourg is a country of under half a million people, three official languages and substantial savoury breakfasts. Jeanne decided early that languages would open the doors to the world. In due course, her interpreting and translating career took her far and wide. One day, she went to Canada in a group led by a young man called Guy who had chosen to be a tour guide because he wanted to do something totally different from his parents.

Jeanne left her job and her country to be with Guy and, despite his earlier vow, together they took over his parents' fishmongery business. For twenty years they lived near Paris and led the tough life of daily market vendors, rising at 2 am to choose the day's fish in Rungis, the wholesale market ("the largest market in the world and the largest port in France" says Jeanne), finishing at 1 pm when the street stalls were dismantled for the day. Although they shared a delight in good food and belonged to a wine-tasting club, it was a stressful life with antisocial hours. The love of travel and meeting new people was still alive, they remembered their B&B experiences as being especially enriching moments during those journeys, and they eventually decided to sell up and go south to adventure, a B&B of their own with superb Luxembourg-style breakfasts, and table d'hôtes, of course.

Their commitment to sustainable, eco-friendly fishing practices had grown as their time in the business came to an end and the fishing industry entered its current crisis. "You will never ever find farmed fish at our table, we only serve wild,

unthreatened species. Most of the short-sighted industry still refuses regulation, yet scallop fishing is a fine example of how things can work: strict rules have been firmly applied and the result is much bigger harvests. Unregulated industrial fishing is killing the Mediterranean."

Guy and Jeanne house-hunted for a year and chose Rocbaron on their first visit. "It was love at first sight, so here we are in Provence, halfway between the Mediterranean and the lovely Lac de Sainte Croix, near the stunning Verdon gorges." Originally a shepherd's house, La Maison de Rocbaron is a typical Provençal village house that they have renovated with a light hand and

> "Their commitment to sustainable, eco-friendly fishing practices grew as their time in the business came to an end and the fishing industry entered its current crisis"

reclaimed materials. The previous owner was in the French navy and the locals still call it "the admiral's house", though his was not in fact so exalted a rank. He used to hold stupendous parties when home on leave and the sense of hospitality is still palpable, if less raucous. Again, Jeanne says: "we both love receiving guests and cooking is my greatest pleasure, I simply revel in it. My father, a true gourmet, started taking me to restaurants when I was ten..."

As long-standing members of Slow Food and engaged in the organic movement, they use fresh local ingredients only and research their sources minutely, buying from nearby market gardeners and organic shops. In five years, they have established what they call "sustainable relationships" with the gardeners, who consider them valuable, if demanding, clients. Rocbaron is ten kilometres from Solliès-Pont, the French fig capital, and Jeanne has made the glorious black fig of Solliès one of her

specialities, adapting it inventively to many dishes. She takes the time to get the culinary detail right while Guy deals with the wine, which comes from a local organic wine-grower; "it's much easier not to spray the vines here; there is so little rain that mildew is rare."

"We are particularly proud of our table d'hôtes. For us, it's essential to the spirit that everyone be at one big table and that we dine with our guests. This is the moment when real contact is made, even lasting friendships. I prefer to give children an early supper so that dinner can be a refined, adult opportunity to discover more sophisticated tastes." They are part of the Sentinel group in their Slow Food convivium, supporting species that are threatened with extinction. Jeanne loves the type of spelt called 'petit épeautre de Haute Provence'. Grown here for 10,000 years then almost killed off in the twentieth century by high-productivity wheats, it has only just been resuscitated. "Its dark, compact flour has a warm, rich taste that is full of personality and never bitter."

The garden has some magnificent old trees – so many that they can't use solar panels to heat the pool. There's no room for a potager, either, much to their regret. Guy does all the weeding by hand, an enormous job, and cleans the swimming pool daily to keep chemical cleaners to a minimum. Here and there, a ceramic or wood-carved face peers at you from a bush, the work of Guy and Jeanne's elder daughter from her time at the Steiner school (she now works in a law firm in Paris). The whole place, with the house a quiet symphony of pink, white and beige, seems to be in harmony with itself and the world.

Jeanne Fischbach & Guy Laguilhemie

La Maison de Rocbaron,
3 rue St Sauveur, 83136 Rocbaron
- 5: 3 doubles, 2 suites.
- €80–€115.
- Dinner with wine, €38.
- +33 (0)4 94 04 24 03
- www.maisonderocbaron.com
- Train station: Toulon

Ardenne   Lorraine   Rhône Valley - Alps

[THE EAST]

In late October, I found the foliage at the peak of its blazing farewell. On the highest slopes there was a chilly breeze but with a limestone wall on my right, the sun pouring down from my left, I strolled along in a t-shirt. In five days of hiking I ran into only four climbers, three hunters out stalking hare and grouse, and four people playing with parapentes.

David Roberts
Alone among the angels

The Alps the youngest, highest and largest mountain range in Europe, form France's borders with Switzerland and Italy. The Duchy of Savoy, guardian of the Alpine passes, had a powerful hand in European dynastic dealings until it became the ball in a game of Franco-Italian ping-pong, ending the match on the French side and becoming Savoie and Haute Savoie. This is dairy land and transhumance is still a reality. The high pastures are not just pretty Heidi stories, they cover half the farmland of the two départements, home to thousands of grazing cows, sheep and goats and almost thirty cheese dairies in summer. A new arrangement brings a few hundred heifers down to the Var to graze the forest undergrowth during the winter and contribute to fire prevention there. This is big-scale sustainable farming.

The Alps impress at all times. Whatever you are doing, be it walking in summer, skiing like mad in winter, climbing any time, fishing and boating on the lakes, or careering down rivers on rafts, their beauty is inescapable.

Ardennes The mountains, lakes and forests of the Ardennes, named after Arduinna, the Celtic warrior goddess whose emblem was the wild boar, straddle the borders with Belgium and Luxemburg. The choice of patroness was prophetic: from that distant time until the birth of the European Union, the region was crossed and re-crossed by warriors.

Arduinna's wild boar is alive and well in her woods today - and is a prized dish throughout north-eastern France, being marinaded with prunes or port, roasted or cooked in a pie, served with cranberries or chestnuts or gherkins. Rimbaud, the poet adventurer, was born in Charleville and fought his demons and the spirit of war in poetry, becoming one of the leading sources of literary modernity before dying young after some sombre business dealings in Egypt.

Lorraine The bucolic pastures of Lorraine lie among slow curves of woods, fields and lakes that have changed little since Joan of Arc was born of peasant parents in 1412. She first heard 'her voices' at Domrémy and was destined to move great men and armies into action then die a martyr to international politics. The rural surface of Lorraine hides a strong industrial current. Steel was king here for 150 years (the steel for the Eiffel Tower was made near Nancy). Lorraine was second only to the US for its iron ore and forests still cover one third of the territory. Nancy's prosperity translated into an elegant and beautiful city of eighteenth-century mansions and two hundred years later nourished the explosion of Art Nouveau, gaining the finest body of Art Nouveau in France.

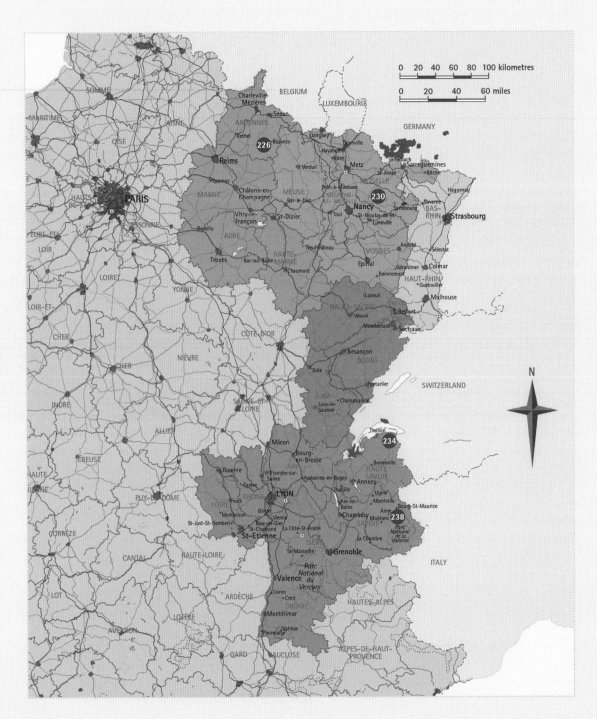

Special places to stay

La Montgonière

CHAMPAGNE - ARDENNE

Élisabeth de Montgon has the history of her family, the Ardennes and France at her fingertips, and that means a lot of knowledge and understanding. The thick woods and abrupt riverside cliffs, the tranquil pastures and little old towns of this quiet region belie its dense and bloody past, thick as it is with memories of marching regiments, invasions and battles of horrific proportions. La Montgonière, Élisabeth's family house, was occupied by German officers three times in seventy years. The second time, in 1914, it was requisitioned for the son of Emperor Wilhelm. No hard feelings, though: she has named one of her bedrooms La Chambre du Prince in memory of this long-gone event.

The village mansion was built in 1673 for a Catholic prelate but the French Revolution, which viewed the high clergy as severely as it did the aristocracy, stripped the occupant of his titles and privileges and confiscated his house. Meanwhile, Élisabeth's ancestors were being thrown into prison and their family château destroyed.

Once the uproar and tragedies were over, history redealt the cards and a Montgon survivor took up with Napoleon Bonaparte. He served in every single one of Napoleon's many campaigns, won the Légion d'Honneur at the battle of Austerlitz (Napoleon's victorious answer to the defeat at Trafalgar)

and moved into this "modest family dwelling" (it only has eight bedrooms, after all). That was over two hundred years ago and the house and family name have been handed down, mostly through the female line, ever since.

Élisabeth moved here after living for many years in the Auvergne, bringing with her a lawyer's quick organising mind, an interest in local politics and a wide-ranging art collection. She loves this "house of women and its feminine soul," tends lovingly to its every need, and keeps two cats. To this house she also brings her fine sense of hospitality. "I detest the commercial attitude, my aim is to make friends with people so that they feel they have been coming here for years. I share my house and the things I know with them and let them discover the area freely."

The first outside space is the manicured, miniature 'château' garden where open lawns and secret bowers, trimmed hedges, shady drives and a very special pond, said to house two otters, make for dreamy relaxation. "And," says Élisabeth, "outside the village there are hundreds of hectares with nothing but woods and wildlife, grazing cattle and the famous Ardennais heavy horses." Mentioned in Caesar's 'Gallic Wars' and recorded as being ridden to Jerusalem in the First Crusade, these wonderful beasts are part of local history. "Wild boar and deer

are much hunted here, with guns and with bows and arrows," she continues, 'but our village of sixty souls has forbidden hunting (I sit on the town council) and my pond is attracting more and more wild duck. We do believe we are making a difference for wildlife." She is on the national heritage committee, too, and is helping to plan a nature discovery trail all round the nearby ponds.

La Tarte aux Raisins (grape tart)

Shortcrust pastry
1 kg grapes
6 tbsp currant jelly
4 tbsp kirsch

- Blind cook the pastry at thermostat 5/6 for 20 minutes
- Wash and deseed the grapes
- Melt jelly in a small pan then add kirsch
- Remove cooked, browned pastry case from oven and spread a layer of jelly over the bottom
- Position the grapes and brush with remaining jelly
- Serve immediately

For a different look, lay black and white grapes to make four quarters on the pastry.

Her orchard produces great quantities of fruit so she makes all her own jams as well as gathering lavender and lots of grapes. Élisabeth loves spoiling guests with big bowls of cherries or strawberries. Otherwise, vegetables come from farmers' markets, organic wherever possible, and meat from the tranquil beasts grazing out in the fields. Élisabeth is happy in the kitchen, preparing local *boudin blanc* (white pork-based sausage) with apple sauce or fillet of pork with rosemary for her guests.

In the house, each room, apart from the 'Prussian Prince', is named and decorated for a member of her family, Louis Emmanuel of Austerlitz fame being the first. At every corner of the house you meet a new family portrait, another faded old photograph, another piece of memorabilia. It is fascinating and never overdone. Besides the ancestors and old prints, Élisabeth has hung a number of modern originals and the whole place is furnished with marvellous family pieces from down the centuries.

As well as history and her house, Élisabeth's other great love is music. In 2003, she founded a classical music festival, Les Notes d'Argonne, that regularly attracts some of the musical world's big names for performances in churches and châteaux in the area. The musicians stay at La Montgonière for the week and a few music-loving B&B guests may be fortunate enough to stay with them. Another string to her bow is the chairmanship of the regional chamber orchestra that specialises in Monteverdi and Bach. This is a supremely cultured and refined place to stay and be nurtured body and soul by an exceptional woman.

Élisabeth Regnault de Montgon

La Montgonière
1 rue St Georges, 08240 Harricourt
- €90–€140.
- 2 doubles, 1 suite for 3–4.
- Dinner €25. Wine extra.
- +33 (0)3 24 71 66 50
- www.lamontgoniere.net
- Train station: Reims

Château d'Alteville

LORRAINE

En passant par la Lorraine,
avec mes sabots,
Rencontrai trois capitaines...
(Passing through Lorraine in my clogs,
I met three captains...)

The lilting folksong, sung by all French children, that inspired Georges Brassens' *Les sabots d'Hélène*, tells of Lorraine's pastoral and military past. Beautiful, wooded, river-run Lorraine, so often a battlefield, its steel industry a twentieth-century victim of globalisation, now displays the quiet optimism of those who have lived through terrible struggles and survived. Off the beaten track, its treasures are largely undiscovered, yet Nancy is a pearl of eighteenth-century architecture and one of the cradles of Art Nouveau. The gothic cathedral of Metz has wonderful windows by Chagall and Cocteau's only creations in stained glass flood the church of St Maximin with blue light. In 2010, Metz leaps into the twenty-first century with the opening of the Centre Pompidou-Metz, an ultra-modern building for exhibitions of contemporary art and cultural events from all over the world.

The countryside around Tarquimpol teems with game, lakes for fishing and fun, forests for the timber industry and long walks. David's firm, led by a committed environmentalist and consultant to the European Commission, works with the authorities to develop the region's rural areas sustainably

and profitably. "Sustainability is automatically part of our advice on joined-up development: all parties, big and small, young and old, must be engaged or it just won't work." Lucky enough to work from home, he is also mayor of tiny Tarquimpol.

As you arrive at Château d'Alteville a sense of continuity envelopes you. The estate is a long-standing family affair with David, Agnieszka and the children in the wing with their B&B guests; his parents, pioneers of B&B in Lorraine and helping with their two grandchildren, in another wing of the château; his brother in the farmhouse opposite, running the organic beef farm; and a sister next door. "A close community that's open to the outside world," is how David describes it.

Proud of the family heritage, he keeps the house in proper château style – beautiful carpets, big paintings, sculptures, antiques – and dinner in the grand dining room is at a long table laid with fine china from Lunéville, glasses from Baccarat and the family silver. They did, tactfully, exchange the stuffed beasts on the walls for photographs of the same animals alive. David and Agnieszka (baby permitting) dine with guests, leading lively conversations about the house and its past occupants, including the Germans during both world wars. David's passion for the Lorraine and the environment, his house and local history, and Agnieszka's happy conversion from Polish city sparrow to deep-country swan – "town-dwellers are often more isolated than I am here," she says – are enough to keep anyone fascinated all evening. It looks grand but there's nothing stuffy or intimidating about place or people.

Leg of wild Alteville boar in red wine

1 leg of wild boar (or vension)
3 tbsp oil
50g butter
1 small glass brandy
1 clove garlic, peeled
50 cl red wine
Juice of 1 lemon
1 chilli
1 tbsp flour
1 tbsp Dijon mustard
Cranberries
Blackcurrant jelly
Salt and pepper

- Heat butter and oil in an iron pot and brown meat on all sides
- Heat brandy
- Drain oil from pot and return meat, pour brandy over meat and set alight, cover pot and cook over low heat for 40 minutes
- Add half the red wine, lemon juice, garlic, chilli, salt and pepper
- Cover and cook for 40 more minutes over low heat
- In bowl, mix mustard and flour with a little red wine
- Pour over contents of pot with remaining red wine
- Stir and cook slowly for at least 3 more hours
- Lay meat on dish with cranberries and serve with sauce and blackcurrant jelly separately
  Even better re-heated.

Agnieszka and David both do the cooking. It's mainly regional food but Agnieszka makes the

occasional Polish dish, such as a beetroot purée that goes wonderfully with game; her 'mirabelle' (cherry plum) tarts, a local speciality, are delicious. David goes for the fish and slow-cook meat recipes – home-grown beef or lamb, game shot on the estate, fish from Alteville's big pond or the surrounding lakes where the wild fish are neither bred nor fed artificially. His wild boar in red wine is memorably succulent. Many vegetables and fruits are grown in the chateau's potager and orchard and the brothers 'do' two pigs a year, exchanged for half a cow with a pig-breeding neighbour. The pigs are transformed on the spot – it takes at least a week – into smoked hams, pâtés, Lorraine sausages, brawn; absolutely nothing is thrown away.

After dinner, David serves his homemade mirabelle brandy with coffee in the salon. Eco-minded guests can also discuss the merits of geothermal as compared to solar or wood-fired heating and admire these conscientious people for choosing cables instead of wireless to distribute the internet around the house because of possibly damaging radio waves.

To walk this all off the next morning, there's a good distance round the Étang de Lindre, visible from the château. Its vast wetlands attract some 250 species of migrating birds. Monsieur Barthélémy senior was instrumental in setting up the excellent information centre on the Tarquimpol promontory and David is actively engaged in keeping farmers and conservationists in agreement on how to make the area work for everyone.

A place of interest and value to stay sustainably and discover a magnificent, little-sung region.

David & Agnieszka Barthélémy

Château d'Alteville,
Tarquimpol, 57260 Dieuze

- 5: 4 doubles, 1 twin.
- €68-€91.
- Dinner €31-€38.50. Wine €10.
- +33 (0)3 87 05 46 63l
- Train station: Salbris

Chalet Châtelet

RHÔNE VALLEY - ALPS

The winding drive through the green mountains is spectacular. The chalet stands alone in the hand of nature, gazing magnificently down the pine-covered lap of the lush Vallée d'Abondance, one of the most unspoilt in the Alps.

The spot has been called Le Châtelet for centuries: a castle was recorded as being in ruins here in 1555. Its panoramic plateau has sun all year, to feed body, soul and solar-powered energy systems. These generate enough power to run much of the house and spa equipment.

"The Slow spirit?" ponders Suzie, "I can't remember not thinking this way. As a post-war child, I grew up with rationing, frugality and a caring attitude to resources. When Pascal and I finally came together as a couple – we met in our teens, on the beach at Eastbourne, believe it or not, then led parallel lives with careers and children for thirty years – we wanted to make sure we got this bit right.

We both loved nature and snow, Abondance and its name full of promise. We had been committed to sustainability long before the word was invented, so we set out to build an earth-respecting family house here, out of conviction and not because it was fashionable." Pascal did lots of research into the *maison éternelle* and the techniques that have lasted for centuries. The finished product is pretty enough to be a picture postcard but they admit that being eco-virtuous meant a long hard haul and living in a caravan for two years.

The house is a model of the latest environmental techniques married to age-old craftsmanship. It is also a traditional shingle-roofed mountain chalet, designed within local building rules which specify that whole logs are forbidden on the outside, they have to be flat-sided. The work was done by a clutch of master craftsmen and looks as if it's been part of the landscape for generations.

Thick sheep's-wool insulation lies between the tree trunks lining the interior. The logs were cut at over 1,300 metres – lower down the trees grow too fast and the timber isn't strong enough – and the frame was pre-assembled there to give the joints time to stretch and shrink. "He shaped those joints the old way, by hand, with compass and saw for perfect dovetailing." The frame was then numbered, dismantled, taken down to Le Châtelet and rebuilt. The local carpenter turned the beautifully smooth staircase and the master stonemason, who normally does church and historical building renovations, left esoteric symbols outside to protect the house and its occupants.

After the builders, the whole family – Suzie and Pascal have five children between them – joined in flooring, tiling and decorating the interior. Then they furnished it, enchantingly, with reclaimed and renovated furniture from a local brocante market – an old oak chest, a cherrywood table, a French armoire – and made it into a family art gallery: Suzie has always painted, her daughter is a sculptor, her son an artist and designer. The atmosphere is that of a well-loved house that's been in the family for decades: comfortable, understated and entirely without swank. A huge Finnish wood-burning stove pumps out heat and cosiness.

Pascal, who knows all the paths, pistes and wildlife, makes it easy for people to come without cars, collecting them from the airport or the station in his minibus and ferrying them around. "That way," he says, "we can show them our lovely secret places to paint, walk, ski or sightsee. There are gorgeous birds and butterflies, some of them rare and famous, the Tengmalm owl for example, or the Azuré de la Noisette butterfly and, though you seldom see them, you can hear the ibex goats shouting at each other from mountain to mountain." Lamartine's butterfly words ring true up here:

S'enivrer de parfums, de lumière et d'azur...

(Drunk on scents, light and azure skies).

Suzie's great pleasure is cooking and serving tasty range-cooked meals to gatherings of people from all horizons while engaging them in wide-ranging talk of

art, theatre, travel and, of course, sustainable living. She gets the local trademark cheese Tomme d'Abondance from the farm next door ("because it's the best"), France's best poultry from nearby Bresse, crayfish and féra fish from Lake Geneva, squashes, spinach, leeks and flowers from her kitchen garden, and potatoes when she manages to save them from the wild boar who relish them. She's very pleased with her raised beds within railway sleeper walls because "slugs are lazy beasts and don't bother to climb the walls." When winter leaves a metre of snow, she goes to her favourite stalls at the market.

She and Pascal positively fizz with enthusiasm for their new life. "We're pretty old-fashioned really: reluctant web-users, minimal telly-watchers, we love walking, gardening and reading. However," she says, "we have done and still do our slow best but we can't change our normal lives to be pure. We're not jumping on any bandwagon, we were on the road before the first Slow one started to roll."

Pascal & Suzie Immediato

Chalet Châtelet,
Route d'Abondance, 74360 Bonnevaux
- 4: 2 doubles, 2 triples.
- €90–€190.
- Dinner with wine, €30.
- +33 (0)4 50 73 69 48
- www.chalet-chatelet.com
- Train station: Thonon les Bains

Maison Coutin

RHÔNE VALLEY – ALPS

There is natural generosity about this open and welcoming family. Backed by incomparable Alpine beauty, the friendly, flower-decked old mountain farmhouse with its shingled roof and view-filled rooms is warm and homely. Claude grew up here until she was spotted as a possible downhill ski racer and sent to a special boarding school. "When I found that ski racing didn't suit me," Claude explains, "I went to explore the wide open spaces of Australia, learning and teaching for five years. But teaching didn't suit me either – not enough patience – and I came home. My parents had started doing B&B, so I started doing table d'hôtes. A few guests were brave enough to try it, then more, then all of them: I had found the thing that suited me and I still revel in it." At twenty-seven, she went to a high-school reunion, and so did Franck. They had never met at school; now he came to join her in Maison Coutin.

Franck learned 'green' building from a builder who used old-style materials and techniques. Now, timber, hemp, sheep's wool and the wood-chip boiler keep the big house cosy at 1,300 metres and solar panels heat the water. He knows the paths and ski slopes of the Tarentaise valley 'like his pocket' and can guide you over the mountains on skis or snowshoes or walk you to his favourite summer picnic spots. In winter, he is a 'piste-basher', a job of skill and daring that involves going out at nightfall with hooks and winches and a snowcat machine to groom the steepest ski trails for several hours. In summer, the family's three kitchen gardens keep him busy until it's time to get the wood-fired oven going for the evening's pizza or fruit tart. This is where the bread is cooked, and the croissants and cakes for breakfast. "The oven is Franck's job," says Claude. "He built it himself and as I am one foot shorter than he is I can't reach it." After homemade aperitifs

(possibly walnut, lemon and cherry leaf), dinners round the big table are high-spirited affairs, the plates stacked with the fruits of this tireless couple's labours. The children will have supped earlier – Franck makes their pizzas with whatever they ask for – and gone to bed or to play with the junior Coutin-Chenals.

"From mountain to valley," says Claude, "our *terroir** produces a rich choice of vegetables and fruit, the famous Beaufort cheese – 'the prince of gruyères' – and meat, milk and yogurt from the cattle and pigs you see in the summer pastures. I buy a whole wheel of Beaufort in the autumn and it lasts us through the winter but the summer vegetables that I preserve in jars run out before the next crop is ripe." This means shopping. "We are keen followers of the idea 'consume as much as possible from within a radius of a hundred kilometres' and we make it as organic as our budget will allow. If I won the lottery, I would go one hundred percent organic for the rest of my life."

Claude's Cabbage Lasagne

- Make a good meat sauce of onions, tomatoes, minced beef and pork and thyme
- Make a white cheese sauce with Beaufort cheese
- Blanch several large cabbage leaves to use instead of lasagne slices
- Spread in successive layers in an oven dish, top with cheese and bake in oven, wood-burning if possible

Although she doesn't eat cheese, she regularly produces a 'raclette' (Raclette cheese melted in a special table oven and eaten with ham and steamed potatoes), or a baked Reblochon 'tartiflette' (virtually the same ingredients but differently cooked), or a 'fondue savoyarde' (four varieties of mountain cheese combined in a communal dipping pot). "I don't use sophisticated recipes, they just don't

work for me. High-quality ingredients and unfussy preparation are the secrets of good healthy food."

Franck keeps bees, parking his hives on the mountain in summer, in the valley in winter. "We have wonderful honey here. There's no rampaging bee sickness in Savoie because crops don't grow at this altitude, only cows, pigs and goats, so the bees' feeding grounds aren't covered in death-dealing pesticides." In the garden, Claude has her own anti-slug weapon: "We use ash from our fires, its cheaper and cleaner than slug pellets; beer put next to lettuces works, too." There are more thrilling sorts of wildlife than garden pests: deer, mountain goats, even a resident eagle.

With all this, plus award-winning flower displays, Claude still finds time to ski. The whole family are *sportifs*. They all run – some have entered half-marathons – and call themselves a team of six, meaning the children, Boris, Clémence and Édouard, ranging from seventeen to seven, the parents, and Ekiden the dog. "Ekiden," Claude tells us, "is the Japanese word for a long-distance relay race or for the final member of a team of relay marathon runners. He's a gun dog, really, but only hunts when Franck tells him; he can eat from the poultry trough without threatening the birds." The children are keen kayak paddlers, too, and snow sports have no secrets for them.

All this talent, energy and commitment might be daunting to the naturally slothful, but it needn't be. They have a wonderful ability to make everyone feel at ease.

Claude Coutin & Franck Chenal

Maison Coutin, 73210 Peisey Nancroix
• 3: 1 triple, 2 suites (1 for 4, 1 for 4-6).
• €54-€60.
• Dinner with wine, €19. Children €6-€11. Restaurant 200 metres .
• +33 (0)4 79 07 93 05
• www.maison-coutin.fr
• Train station: Bourg St Maurice

Notes and explanations

WWOOF is a worldwide network of national organisations that match organic farmers with volunteers (Wwoofers) who come to live and learn on the farms. As well as helping each other to make a healthier world, hosts and volunteers promote cultural understanding of the many diverse peoples and cultures around the world as they share their daily lives. Not only young people join the scheme. Others may come for a career break, or to find an alternative to their ordinary 'high-street' life and to reconnect with nature and perhaps, even, with lost ideals – a way to Go Slow.

LPO

Ligue de Protection des Oiseaux
www.lpo.fr

Similar to Britain's RSPB, the LPO seeks to protect endangered bird species, to limit the ill effects of shooting for sport and to promote bio-diversity.

ASPAS

Association pour la Protection des Animaux Sauvages
www.aspas-nature.org

NGO whose mission is to protect French wildlife and help landowners to establish animal sanctuaries on their land. It supports organic farming and gardening and condemns the indiscriminate use of chemicals on the land.

GRETIA

Groupe d'Etude des Invertébrés Armoricains
www.gretia.org

Based in north-west France (*Armorique*); particularly concerned with the protection of grasshoppers, spiders, butterflies, etc, which are losing species every year; advises landowners on, for example, creating a butterfly sanctuary on their land: how to do without chemicals, what to grow to promote reproduction, what dried plants not to cut down to avoid destroying the larvae's hibernation spots.

Kokopelli

A French association that sells organically and bio-dynamically-grown seeds. Its purpose is to help protect bio-diversity with much of its focus on Third World needs. Since 1992, it has concentrated on vegetable varieties (marrows, aubergines, tomatoes, peppers...). Intensive, chemical-centred agriculture is fast reducing the number of varieties in existence and creating seeds that do not reproduce themselves.

Small peasant farmers are taken hostage by this system. Traditionally, they will sow next year the seeds from this year's crop; they cannot afford to buy new seeds for every harvest. The potential for varieties to change, mutate and reproduce must be preserved for future generations. Kokopelli's European members grow seeds of rare and fast-disappearing varieties both for themselves and for distribution in Third World countries where traditional varieties have been lost through intensive farming and western-driven 'improvement' schemes (India, South America, etc).

Kokopelli also nurtures the creation of peasant-farmer networks and genetic resource centres in the Third World whereby the farmers can keep or take back control of their own livelihoods.

La Semaine du Goût - The Taste Week

In 1990, under the aegis of the Sugar Collective (sic), the first Taste Day saw 350 chefs give groups of 8-9 year-old Paris schoolchildren the first organised 'lessons in taste'. The Day became The Week and The Week became a nationally-recognised event. Organised each October, it is used as a welcome platform by hundreds of primary-school teachers.

The operation grew bigger and is now in the capable hands of the Ministry of Agriculture, Food, Fishing and Rural Affairs. Many famous and soon-to-be-famous chefs participate every year, giving "lessons in taste" in public places (audiences have made astonishing discoveries) and in schools across the country. Some top-class restaurants offer special low-cost Taste-Day menus. Last but not least, the event has recently been promoting home cooking, encouraging people to do it themselves and 'develop their taste.'

Terroir

The word has been used for centuries to mean a piece of land considered for its agricultural potential. People as well as products can be *du terroir*. Not long ago, it carried a whiff of country-bumpkinism - it still implies the local, the traditional, the unmodernised - but it has always been most widely used to identify and distinguish small patches of wine-growing land, except in Burgundy where the word *climat* is used to mean much the same thing.

In the world of wine-growing, great wines are often grown in surprisingly small vineyards. Each of these has specific terroir characteristics which are a combination of natural factors: the geology (the underlying rock), the soil, the altitudude, the orientation, the climate and the micro-climate (one side of a hill can have a different climate from the other). One way to get the feel is to look at your own garden and notice what does well where and how things can change for a plant if you simply move it to the other side.

In the last decade or two terroir has been recruited into the service of all sorts of artisan, locally-produced foods, almost coming to mean the opposite of 'processed' or 'industrial'.

Bicycling in France

Two and a half times the size of Great Britain and about the size of Texas, France offers rich rewards to the cyclist: plenty of space, a superb network of minor roads with little traffic, and a huge diversity of landscapes, terrains and smells (smell contributes so much to the pleasure of riding through the countryside). You can chose the leafy forests and undulating plains of the north, or the jagged glacier-topped mountains of the Alps. Pedal through wafts of fermenting grapes in Champagne, resinous pines in the Midi, or spring flowers in the Pyrenees. You can amble slowly, stopping in remote villages for delicious meals or a café au lait, or pit yourself against the toughest terrains and cycle furiously. Or you can plan to 'do' all the châteaux of the Loire, one after the other. Once you're in France, it is useful to know that, although the proper academic name for the "little queen", as fond users call it, is 'une bicyclette', it is always known as 'un vélo'.

You will be joining in a national sport: bicycling is an important part of French culture and thousands don their lycra and take to their bikes on summer weekends for a family ride or a serious race. The country comes to a virtual standstill during the three-week Tour de France bike race in July and cycling stars become national heroes with quasi-divine status. Their misdeeds and downfalls, physical or moral, are as important as those of Europe's royals and other objects of the celebrity cult.

When to go
Avoid July and August, if possible, as it's hot and the roads are at their busiest. The south is good from mid-March, though high ground may hold snow until the end of June. The north can be lovely from May onwards. Most other areas are suitable from April until October.

Getting bikes to and through France
You can get your bicycle to France prettily easily. Ferries carry bikes for nothing or for a small fee. On Eurostar, you should be able to store them in one of the guards' vans, just book ahead and 'buy your bike a ticket'.

Some mainline and most regional trains accept bikes, for a fee. Information on timetables is contradictory and ticket agents may not have up-to-date information so be certain, check up at the station the day before you set off. Insist on a ticket *avec réservation d'un emplacement vélo*. If you are two or more, make sure the booking is multiple. In the Paris area, you can take bikes on most trains except during rush hours.

Maps
The two big names are Michelin and the Institut Géographique National (IGN). For route-planning, IGN publishes a map of the whole of France showing mountain-biking and cycle tourism. The best on-the-road reference maps are Michelin's yellow 1:200,000 Series. IGN publishes a Green Series to the scale of 1:100,000. For larger scale maps, go for IGN's excellent 1:25,000 Top 25 and Blue Series (which you will also use for walking).

A map of Paris showing bike routes, one-way streets, bus sharing lanes, long-term rental facilities (Maison Roue Libre), weekend pedestrian and bike-only streets is available at some bookshops. Order it on line: www.media-cartes.fr

Useful contacts

- Fédération Française de Cyclotourisme. For cyclists and mountain bikers. www.ffct.org

- Fédération Française de la Randonnée Pédestre (FFRP). Leading organisation for walkers and ramblers. Their guide books are useful for cyclists, too, and many of them have been translated into English. www.ffrp.asso.fr

- SNCF (French Railways) www.voyages-sncf.com

Bike hire

Consult the owners of the place you are staying at about local bike hire.

Cycling in French cities
Municipal hire schemes

- Paris: Velib' www.velib.paris.fr

In 2007, the Paris council launched its bike rental scheme with 1,200 'stations', each holding a dozen solidly-built bikes for €1 per day, €5 per week, €29 per year, payable by credit card. The first half hour of each new rental period is included in the charge.

- Many other French cities run bike-hire schemes: consult each city's website.

Walking in France

With over 60,000km of clearly marked long-distance footpaths, or *sentiers de Grande Randonnée* (GRs for short), and a fantastic array of landscapes and terrains, France is a superb country for walking. Hike in the glaciers of the Northern Alps, walk through the lush then rugged volcanic 'moonscapes' of the Auvergne, or amble through the vineyards of Burgundy, Alsace or Provence.

Stroll for an afternoon, or make an odyssey of several months. Some long-distance walks are classics: the famous GR65, the pilgrim path to Santiago de Compostela, the Tour du Mont Blanc, or the 450-kilometre GR3 *Sentier de la Loire*, which runs the length of France's longest river from Ardèche to the Atlantic. Wild or tamed, hot or temperate, populated or totally empty – France has it all.

Wherever you stay, there will almost certainly be a GR nearby. You can walk a stretch of it, then use other paths to turn it into a circular walk. As well as the network of GRs, marked with red and white stripes, there are Petite Randonnée (PRs), usually identified by single yellow or green stripes. In addition, there are sentiers de *Grande Randonnée de Pays* (GRPs), marked by a red and yellow stripe, and any number of variants of the original GR route which have become paths in their own right. Hiking trails and walking paths are evolving all the time.

The paths are lovingly waymarked and maintained by the Fédération Française de la Randonnée Pédestre (FFRP) who also publish Topo-Guides (see Books).

The great reward if you walk is that you penetrate the soul of rural France as you never could from a car. You'll see quaint ruined châteaux, meet unforgettable country characters and see a dazzling variety of flora and fauna if you take the time to look. France has a rich natural heritage, including 266 species of nesting birds, 131 species of mammals and nearly 5,000 species of flowering plants. Look out for golden eagles, griffon vultures and marmots in the Alps and Pyrenees, red kites and lizard orchids in the Dordogne, fulmars and puffins off the rocky coast of Brittany. Hundreds of species are threatened with extinction, however: 400 species of flora and about 20 species of mammals and birds are vulnerable or endangered.

When to go

The best months are May, June, September and October. In high mountain areas, summers are briefer and paths may be free of snow only between July and early September. In northern France, July and August are also good months; southern France is ideal for a winter break: days are often crisp and clear, if shorter.

Maps

The two big names for maps are IGN (Institut Géographique National) and Michelin. IGN maps are of most use for walkers. IGN Grande Randonnée sheet No. 903 with all the long-distance footpaths is good for planning walks. For walking, the best large-scale maps are IGN's 1:25,000 Série Bleue and Top 25 series. Also look out for IGN's 1:50,000 Loisirs de Plein Air series which includes GRs and PRs, plus hotels and campsites for a few areas.

Books

The FFRP produces over 180 Topo-Guides for walkers with instructions and IGN maps. There are

PR (petite randonnée) guides for one-day walks and GR (grande randonnée) guides for walks with at least one overnight. Most are now in English, too, so buy the ones you need before leaving.

Website

Fédération Française de la Randonnée Pédestre (FFRP) Leading organisation for walkers and ramblers. Many of their guide books have been translated into English. www.ffrp.asso.fr

Trains

To get to your starting point by train, the most user-friendly website is www.raileurope.com.

The Code du Randonneur (The Walker's Code)

- Love and respect nature
- Avoid unnecessary noise
- Destroy nothing
- Do not leave litter
- Do not pick flowers or plants
- Do not disturb wildlife
- Shut all gates behind you
- Protect and preserve the habitat
- No smoking or fires in the forests
- Stay on the footpath
- Respect and understand country people and their way of life
- Think of others as you think of yourself

National & Regional
Nature Parks & Hôtels au Nature

7 National Parks (one opening end 2010)
48 Regional Nature Parks

The idea of national parks saw the light in France in 1960, the Vanoise national park was created in 1963 and General de Gaulle signed the initial legislation in 1967. In 2010, national and regional nature parks represent eleven percent of the country's landmass: there are fifty-five of them. Most are off the beaten track and are often missed by the foreign visitor. The motorway network is such that one swishes past huge swathes of beautiful countryside without even realizing it.

The National and Regional Nature Parks are run by separate bodies, the 'national' by a ministry, the 'regional' by a federation, but they are together in promoting:

- Protection and management of France's natural and cultural heritage
- Participation in town and country planning and management of sustainable economic and social development
- Welcoming and informing the public, raising environmental awareness

There is a ban on hunting, camping, building and road construction in the mainland national parks of Les Cévennes, Les Écrins, Mercantour, Port-Cros, Les Pyrénées and La Vanoise (and Les Calanques, near Marseille, opening in 2010). They are closely managed by the central authority and levels of protection and supervision in their heartlands are high. Access can be difficult but the rewards are considerable.

The regional parks are less bound up in red tape than the national parks and their territories represent a looser grouping of interested parties, mainly local authorities, nature-protection groups, residents and tradespeople. Camping sites, gîtes and hotels are permitted, though carefully regulated, and the emphasis is on respect for the special natural environment and promotion of the specific delights of the particular nature park. It is hoped that residents will pay more than simple lip service to the sustainable development ideal so that wilderness and human activity can live comfortably side by side.

There are regional parks in the mountains of Queyras (Hautes Alpes park), the plains of the Vexin (Île de France just north of Paris), along the coast of the Camargue (Provence), in the woodlands in the Northern Vosges (Alsace-Lorraine), in the wetlands of Brière (Western Loire), and many more wild and wonderful places. All are ideal for ramblers and families. Serious walkers can choose from the many sentiers de Grande Randonnée (GR) which cross the parks, and all park offices provide local walking maps.

There are grottoes and museums to visit, animal parks roamed by bison, yak, greater kudu and a pack of wolves, bikes, canoes and kayaks to rent. Other activities include horse-riding, canal boating, sailing, fishing, spa treatments, wine tours, swimming, rock climbing, hand gliding, ballooning. There are packhorses in Livradois-Forez (Auvergne), vultures in Verdon and donkeys for hire in Haut Languedoc. A range of activities make these parks ideal for children and a multitude of crafts are to be observed: clog making, silk weaving and glass working; stone cutting in the Morvan (Burgundy), pipe-making in the Haut Jura (Franche Comté) and cheese-making in several places.

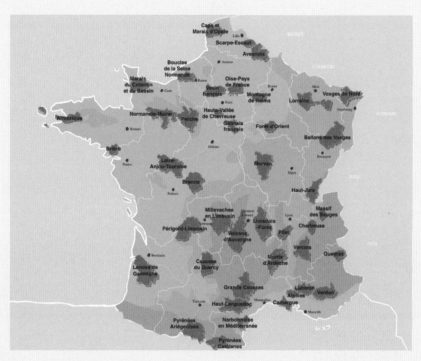

Websites

National Parks: www.parcsnationaux.fr

Regional Parks central website that links to all the parks and has a useful summary in English: www.parcs-naturels-regionaux.tm.fr

Hôtels au Naturel   www.hotels-au-naturel.com

There are, at present, twenty-one hotels in seven regional nature parks that have been admitted to the Hôtels au Naturel charter. This specifies that, as an ambassador of the park where it stands, a Hôtel au Naturel should:

- fit the local style, be it in deep country or on the edge of a village
- have knowledgeable, welcoming staff
- serve food that is carefully made with fresh, local and, ideally, organic produce
- have owners who are committed to their special environment and happily share their love and knowledge of the park, its flora and fauna
- help visitors organize their visits (where to go, what to look for, the unknown paths and secret treasures)
- show their eco-responsibility by taking care over packaging, recycling, water and energy conservation and waste management

Sawday's Fragile Earth series

The Fragile Earth series is a growing collection of campaigning books about the environment and an important part of our company. Highlighting the perilous state of our world yet offering imaginative and radical solutions and some intriguing facts, these books will make you weep and smile. They will keep you up to date and well armed for the battle with apathy.

For many years Sawday's has been 'greening' its business. Our aim is to reduce our environmental footprint as far as possible. (We once claimed to be the world's first carbon-neutral publishing company, but are now wary of such claims.) In recognition of our efforts, we won a Business Commitment to the Environment Award in 2005, and in 2006 a Queen's Award for Enterprise in the Sustainable Development category. In that year Alastair was voted ITN's 'Eco Hero'. In 2008, and again in 2009 we won the Independent Publishing Guild's Environmental Award.

Climate Change
Our Warming World
£12.99

Climate Change — Our Warming World provides a concise and easy to understand summary of climate change covering the causes and impacts of, and solutions to, this global crisis. With powerful images and testimonials written by those already affected, this book offers a critical insight into our changing climate and underlines the need to take action today.

Climate Change aims to inform and inspire immediate action to safeguard our planet, with an introduction by Archbishop Desmond Tutu, a preface by Dale Vince, founder of Ecotricity, and quotes from Dr Pachauri, Chairman of the UN's Intergovernmental Panel on Climate Change, Sir David Attenborough and Susan Sarandon.

To order any of the books in the Fragile Earth series
call +44 (0)1275 395431 or visit www.fragile-earth.com

Stuffed   £14.99
Positive action to prevent a global food crisis

Stuffed presents a global perspective on food production and agriculture and proposes a sustainable and fairly traded path we can follow to secure food for all and protection for the planet.

Money Matters
Putting the eco into economics   £7.99

This well-timed book will make you look at everything from your bank statements to the coins in your pocket in a whole new way. Author David Boyle sheds new light on our money system and exposes the inequality, greed and instability of the economies that dominate the world's wealth.

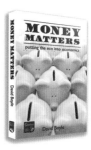

The Book of Rubbish Ideas   £6.99

Every householder should have a copy of this guide to reducing household waste and stopping wasteful behaviour. Containing step-by-step projects, the book takes a top-down guided tour through the average family home.

Do Humans Dream of Electric Cars?   £4.99

This guide provides a no-nonsense approach to sustainable travel and outlines the simple steps needed to achieve a low carbon future. It highlights innovative and imaginative schemes that are already working, such as car clubs and bike sharing.

The Big Earth Book
Updated paperback edition   £12.99

This book explores environmental, economic and social ideas to save our planet. It helps us understand what is happening to the planet today, exposes the actions of corporations and the lack of action of governments, weighs up new technologies, and champions innovative and viable solutions.

Sawday's Special Places to Stay series

RRP £14.99

Italy

Everyone is in love with Italy, aren't they? Or perhaps the idea of it, touted across the centuries by all those poets and painters, photographers, writers and film makers that have entranced us with their romantic words and evocative images. A misty winter morning in watery Venice, a Tuscan hill-top estate dotted with cypress trees, edgy Naples with its sheet-lined streets, Sicilian lemon groves and, of course, rip-roaring Rome with its ancient attractions and crazy driving. But where to stay? Where to find places to match the magnificence of your surroundings? Well, Sawday's of course.

"They only endorse the very best." **The Italian**

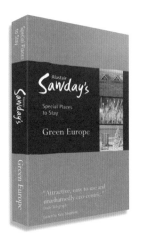

RRP £13.99

Green Europe

Many places call themselves 'eco' or 'green', yet standards differ enormously throughout the world. This guide features very special owners who go the extra mile to provide responsible holidays in Europe. In this new guide you will find special places to stay run by owners who use eco-friendly technologies, contribute to conservation and try to offer something positive to their local communities. There are snow pods, treehouses, yurts, tipis, country B&Bs, organic farmstays and eco-chic hotels. This book also discusses each country's initiatives on 'going green' and provides information on public transport around Europe.

"Sawday is a campaigner for the environment and good food, and his recommendations are like those of a good friend who knows just what sort of place you are looking for." *The Guardian*

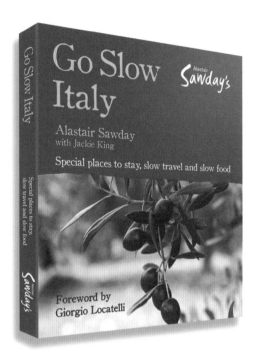 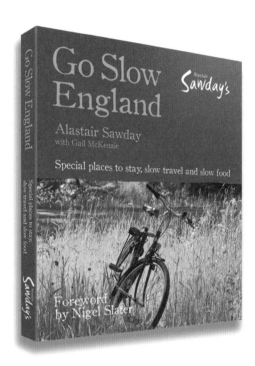

RRP £19.99

The Slow Food revolution is upon us and these guides celebrate the Slow philosophy of life with a terrific selection of the places, recipes and people who take their time to enjoy life at its most enriching. In these beautiful books that go beyond the mere 'glossy', you will discover an unusual emphasis on the people who live in Special Slow Places and what they do. You will meet farmers, literary people, wine-makers and craftsmen – all with rich stories to tell. *Go Slow England, Go Slow Italy* and our new title *Go Slow France* celebrate fascinating people, fine architecture, history, landscape and real food.

"Go Slow England is a magnificent guidebook" *BBC Good Food Magazine*

RRP £19.99. To order any of these titles at the Readers' Discount price of £12.99 (plus p&p) call +44(0)1275 395431 and quote 'Reader Discount GSF'.

To order call 01275 395431 or visit our online bookshop www.sawdays.co.uk/bookshop for up to 40% discount